What I Learned In Life From A Liquid Manure Pit

The Incredible Learning Experiences of Selling Direct to Farmers

By: Stan Barnes
President and Owner—Barnes & Barnes Consulting Group

Copyright © 2009 by Stan Barnes

What I Learned In Life From A Liquid Manure Pit
The Incredible Learning Experiences of Selling Direct to Farmers
by Stan Barnes

Printed in the United States of America

ISBN 978-1-60791-380-1

All rights reserved solely by the author. The author guarantees all contents are original and do not infringe upon the legal rights of any other person or work. No part of this book may be reproduced in any form without the permission of the author. The views expressed in this book are not necessarily those of the publisher.

www.xulonpress.com

1. Forward by—Tony Rubleski—Author, Consultant and Public Speaker.. vii
2. Preface by—Stan Barnes—Author, Consultant and Public Speaker.. xiii
3. About the Author by—Publisher... xi
4. Illustrations by—Paul 'Stretch' Nauta—Retired Wal-Mart Truck Driver

Chapter 1	"You are on your own baby."	17
Chapter 2	"It's no bull selling to farmers and it can be a risky business too."	37
Chapter 3	"Prosperous Cold Calls on farmers you just met for the first time."	43
Chapter 4	"A father and son farming team teach me a lesson I will never forget."	49
Chapter 5	"Former-farmers selling to farmers, were their own worst enemy."	55
Chapter 6	"Persistence in sales pays off in the long run if you live to tell about it."	61
Chapter 7	"Dress for success or at least dress for the part."	67
Chapter 8	"Signs, signs, everywhere there are signs, and most of the time it means pay-dirt, sometimes it means trouble."	71
Chapter 9	"Learning to love the smells you once hated."	75
Chapter 10	"What I learned in life from a liquid manure pit."	81

Chapter 11	"The different things grain, livestock and dairy farmers taught me."	91
Chapter 12	"Guts, persistence and courage can make things happen in your favor."	99
Chapter 13	"You need to find a farmer friend and a banker friend in the township you plan to work."	109
Chapter 14	"Futures, hog bellies, and being talked into something I knew absolutely nothing about."	117
Chapter 15	"Wild times following up Farm Machinery Trade Show leads in the rural parts of Tennessee and Kentucky."	121
Chapter 16	"Silos, equipment, barns and home judging are not all they appear to be."	133
Chapter 17	"Learning the value of having the tools you need in sales to not only get the job done, but excel too."	143
Chapter 18	"Some additional reasons and stories why I loved selling to farmers and why it was so much fun."	147
Chapter 19	"A further sampling of the many great stories I love to share in seminars, parties, and other social gatherings."	153
Chapter 20	"Epilogue."	171

Foreword By: Tony Rubleski
President and owner of Mind Capture Group

When someone takes the time and discipline to write a book, I'm already impressed. Capturing thoughts, ideas, but more importantly stories, is something humans have done for thousands of years via the spoken word, in printed books and now via the Internet. In today's digital world however, storytelling has often been edited down to "made for TV" sound bytes and three-minute videos on YouTube. The next wave of leaders is in such a hurry that I fear they're missing the unique lessons, and wisdom, of well written words. More importantly, they're missing the rich, powerful, and timeless lessons, that stories teach us.

I've been blessed to have met and studied with many sharp and talented folks in my business career, and I must tell you that I consider Stan Barnes first a friend, but more importantly someone who I trust and admire greatly. While there may be 25 or 30 years (I'm sure Stan will dispute this!) difference in our ages, his sage advice and life lessons are timeless and valuable. I'm grateful to have had his ear and soak up his powerful stories and life lessons for the price of a breakfast, when I know clients have willingly paid him hundreds of thousands of dollars over the years.

After one of our power breakfasts last year, I asked him how his book was coming along and I received a sheepish grin. After a bit of pushing and prodding I fired him up and nudged him over the edge to re-engage and set a goal to get the book done. True to his word, Stan didn't disappoint me. What you now hold in your hands is the physical creation of a powerful collection of stories and life lessons that every person can use to not only improve their sales, but more importantly, their life and those they seek to serve.

With up close and personal stories from the field, Stan breaks down the power of persistence, goal-setting, and negotiating in a unique, yet engaging way, based on his many years of selling to farmers in the heartland. As I read story after story I laughed and shook my head in agreement with Stan's comments and viewpoints on what it takes to be successful.

His idea of 'cherry picking' the best accounts is something good marketers do; which we know as vertical marketing. I also found his territory management skills something every sales rep, new or seasoned, should study and use if they want to serve more people each day. Having trained many sales teams, I often find that most of them waste incredible amounts of time each day due to poor scheduling and lack of focus. Stan offers great insights from his own successful career on how to solve this problem.

The visual image and story of Stan running for his life from a huge bull he shares in chapter two, is priceless and may even save your life if you find yourself in a Midwest cornfield soon or in the future. I was in my local Starbuck's reading the manuscript laughing out loud, with the barista girl looking over the coffee machine at me, like I was nuts. You MUST read this for yourself; and all I can say is, I'm glad that Stan's still here today. You could not have made this stuff up.

Another interesting note is that Stan preaches systems in the sales process. I've had the honor of sharing the stage with small business guru Michael Gerber, author of the classic book *The EMyth*, and this is something he preaches as well. Far too many businesses, salespeople, and entrepreneurs miss the power of using systems and often end up out of business within the first three years of opening their doors. It's refreshing to hear from someone who not only believes in it, but more importantly shares how he's used them over the years to achieve success.

I'm often amazed at the lack of discipline and continual struggles most businesses, and sales people in particular, face today because they have little, if any systems in place to insure their success with their sales and marketing. I believe these proven systems are the most important things to have running properly in every top organization.

So there you have it. A collection of powerful stories from Stan that will not only make you laugh, but will also put a smile on your face and your checkbook if you do what he describes. This is a great book by a great guy at the right time in our nation's history, when the economy needs a serious shot in confidence and sales. Read each page with a highlighter in hand and understand that you are being mentored by a master.

Tony Rubleski, #1 Bestselling Author, Consultant and Public Speaker
December 2008 www.MindCaptureBook.com

About The Author

Stan was born and raised in St. Louis, Missouri and tells us he had a joyful and adventuresome childhood. In high school, he excelled as a class clown and a jock, loving every sport but basketball, which he hated. He graduated in the bottom third of his class and he likes to tell people… "I was the third of the class that made the other two thirds possible." He married his high school sweetheart, Judy Ellis, fresh out of high school and they were both 18 years old at the time. Judy and Stan worked their way through college at the University of Missouri in Columbia, Missouri with various jobs and small student loans, plus an occasional care package from home now and then. They are proud to say they paid off their student loans within two years of Stan graduating with a B.A. in communications, speech and broadcasting in January of 1965.

After working a couple of years at the University's owned and operated television station, KOMU-TV, Stan held producer director positions at WFLT-TV in Chicago, Illinois and WOOD-TV in Grand Rapids, Michigan. Then, after a short stint with an advertising and marketing firm, Stan landed a sales rep position with an audio/visual production company that produced promotional films and commercials for corporate 100 companies, and companies with gross sales of just a few million dollars. It was with this firm Stan became directly involved in the very successful sales program which helped him get the offer to become the National Sales Manager of Ace Nut & Bolt Company out of Middleville Michigan.

After the farmer/sales career, Stan returned to the audio/visual production business for a couple of years and also got involved with a company for one year that filmed NASCAR racing around the country. Then on January 1, 1983, he and his wife began Barnes & Barnes Consulting Group. Stan still consults to businesses and trains salespeople. He plans to write a series of books on "What he has learned in life from...." his various experiences and adventures in life.

Preface — By: Stan Barnes

I have been fortunate enough to have a few great mentors come in and out of my life over the years. A couple were clients, and some were family and friends. All of them wanted to help me win in life. Because I have found Eagles fly and think like other Eagles for the most part, as I look back now, much of their great advice to me was similar, while each of them offered me some fresh, new information. Many of my business clients taught me important things on how to run a business successfully too, most of which allowed me to become increasingly successful as a business and sales consultant.

After a lot of priceless experience, I became a consultant specializing in dealing with smaller companies usually not exceeding twenty million in sales annually. While I did work for much larger companies, I found these smaller companies far more rewarding for many reasons including less politics. While politics are always present in any size company or organization, I could deal directly with the owners in these smaller companies. With only a few exceptions, this was almost impossible in larger ones, especially once they got in the 150 million dollar per year range and above.

As I write this book, I am currently working with a number of different types and sizes of companies and nonprofit organizations servicing a wide variety of business fields and community efforts. Over the years, while there have been some narrow escapes, I can proudly say that I've never lost a company I consulted, once they followed the proven advice I gave them to implement.

One of my heroes was Paul "Papa Bear" Bryant. He set records for his victories at various colleges before becoming famous during his great tenure of 25 years of coaching at the University of Alabama. Coach Bryant passed away three weeks after I began my company in January of 1983. I had collected and comprised a list of over 70 words of wisdom from him prior to his passing, and I found a few more afterwards.

One statement from his powerful motivational film, "Nothing But A Winner" became a guiding principle for my method of doing business. He said in that film... *"The same things win for us that always win for us. We just have a whole bunch of excuses as to why we don't use those winning things when we lose."*

One incredible time span in my life, prior to going into the consulting business covers what this book is all about. I have dreamed of writing this book about that period of my life for years. It took place in the early to mid 1970's. I have shared many meaningful and relevant stories about this period in my sales seminars, and I have gotten many laughs in those seminars and in social gatherings along the way too.

This period of my life was the four and a half years I operated as a national sales manager, and later as a distributor/salesperson, for a nut, bolt and tool company that sold direct to farmers, right on their farm, in about twenty of the major farming states. This direct sales approach eliminated the middleman. That saved farmers real money and it made the company I was representing, and me too for that matter, lots of money. In fact, per capita, if you take into consideration inflation, that four and a half years of my life, was the most money I ever made.

What I Learned In Life From A Liquid Manure Pit

About the only thing I knew about farming before I took this position, I had learned from visiting my relative's farms in Illinois and Missouri, and what I saw in the movies and on television. I was amazed to find an entirely new world out there when I began to make my living selling direct to farmers.

I learned to love these wonderful people spread across this great nation of ours. Personally, in my four and a half year tenure, my best estimate is that I probably met from eight to ten thousand of them, on their farms and at conventions and fairs, in about twenty states.

The great experiences and stories I gained during this time in my life remain priceless to me. Now I plan to share these times and experience with you while weaving into the stories, meaningful sales concepts and ideas that work for me to this day. I guarantee you they will work for you too.

When I began my career in business and sales consulting in January of 1983, my background was mostly radio and television, communications, advertising, marketing and audio/visual production. I was convinced I could help companies and organizations be better once I worked with them, so I wrote my personal mission statement to read that way.

I firmly believed that whatever stage a company or organization was in, once I started to work with them, I would be able to help them achieve a higher level of success. In time, this has culminated in me working with hundreds of companies and organizations that ranged from "turn around" situations to those who were already *the market leader,* and wanted to be even better.

However, of all the jobs I had prior to starting my own company, the four and a half years selling direct to farmers gave me *far more valuable experience than any other job I had ever held previously.* To this day, I still use and teach things I learned out there in that great American cropland country of ours, and I share them often.

In my consulting business, I experienced an incredible amount of joy, and a good share of angst and even some tears along the way too. There were times when I was sure the light at the end of the tunnel was a freight train about to wipe me and everybody I was working with, totally off the face of the earth.

In addition, there were times I had individual victories with people who really wanted to go places and succeed. Some of these people allowed me to mentor them as I had been mentored, and many of them have ended up leading some of the finest businesses and organizations around the country. *Therefore, I want you to consider this book as your own private mentor to help you not only to win, but also to excel in everything you do.*

Throughout this book, as I tell my tales and share my adventures, I will highlight some ideas and concepts I have just mentioned. I have always liked that kind of approach in a book that gives you a great assortment of helpful things to learn. It also helps you to review the book quickly after reading a chapter.

Sometimes these highlighted points will be serious; and sometimes they will make you smile. And other times, I expect you will laugh out loud as so many have done before you when I have shared these priceless experiences. I have a lot to share and I do not want you to miss a thing so I hope you enjoy this book as much as I have enjoyed writing it and living it. At the time this all took place in the early to mid 1970's, I was not keeping a journal and I am sorry to say my adventures were not recorded with pictures either. Therefore, while the instances and situations are true, some of the facts, figures and numbers are as close as I can best recall.

Finally, I want to let you know I am dedicating this book to my wife Judy, who is without a doubt the epitome of a successful business leader. She was and still is to this day an incredible CEO of a major organization for 25 years now. She has always been a wonderful loving, caring and supportive wife as well as the mother of our two great daughters Deb and Kim, three fantastic grandchildren Seth, Joe and Anna, and one great grandchild, Cameron. Judy is my best friend, wife and lover of well over 47 years of marriage now, and two years of dating in high school before that. She and I hope and pray to experience many more joyful and fruitful years together. In addition, I am dedicating this book and at least one tenth of the profits to help promote the teachings of our Lord and Savior Jesus Christ, who gave me eternal life, once I accepted His grace.

Chapter 1.

You Are On Your Own Baby

Prior to getting involved in selling to farmers, I need to set the stage as to how it all took place. I had obtained a B.A. in communications and broadcasting from the University of Missouri and I worked at the University owned television station two years before I graduated. During the last two years of my college and after I left college, I held down positions at TV stations in Columbia Missouri, Chicago, Illinois and Grand Rapids, Michigan.

During that time, I became proficient in the development of audio/visual sales, motion picture film, video and slide productions. My reputation for producing results-oriented productions grew to the point that by word of mouth, people sought me out. So before I was enticed to join a company selling to farmers direct from the back of pickup trucks, with camper tops, I was asked to produce a self contained, audio/visual sales program for the same company.

The owner had been frustrated in that his distributors and salespeople around the country were not consistently presenting the company message and the benefits of his program to farmers. He was not sure if the technology existed but he was convinced that once a self-contained A/V sales program was produced by a successful sales person, his distributors and salespeople would dramatically increase sales for themselves, and the company. They would do this by presenting the same message, or proven template, repeatedly. They would then be able to take over and culminate the sales process. That was the challenge Bob, the owner of the company, gave me and the firm I worked for at the time, to accomplish.

We pulled our creative team together and everyone readily accepted the challenge. I think a lot of the enthusiasm had to do with the fact this challenge was so unique and so different from what we were all used to doing on a daily basis. For example, at the time, two of our biggest clients were Amway and Oldsmobile. Our team went to work developing a program that would be a "cutting edge" method of selling direct to the farmer, literally "in the field", off the tailgate of a pickup truck or in the cab.

You never present the exact same presentation twice, but you do need to have a proven sales system or template to guide you. The basic program we produced accomplished this critical goal so well, my company and I gained instant respect with the owner as the additional income began to roll in for him.

I too loved the challenge the owner presented to us. In addition, we were lucky that recently, new audio/visual technology had been developed. It was a portable filmstrip machine with a synchronized audio cassette. It also had two rechargeable batteries. In addition, it had a screen the size of a small TV. With this unit, the sales person could show the presentation to the farmer on the tailgate of his truck, on the farmer's workbench or when the elements were bad, in the cab of his pickup truck.

During the production of the sales program, I developed an instant rapport with Bob, the owner of the company. I also began my real education of farming because most of the program was filmed on location at real farms. One of the more humorous stories of all was the first day of shooting. Because Bob knew farming, he also knew exactly what kind of pictures he wanted in the program to match the written script. The script called for different types of farm equipment to actually be working in the field.

That first day, the script called for a shot of a manure spreader being pulled through a harvested cornfield. Since neither the photographer nor I had been raised on a farm, we got real close to catch the action. The young kid getting ready to start it up for us said… "You guys may want to move back a bit." That's when Bob, the owner of the nut and bolt company said… "Nah, go ahead and get it rolling. They are back far enough and I want them to get some good action shots."

Well, within seconds, we were both covered with manure and everyone had a great laugh at our expense. We did get the shots we needed since the Nikon camera we were using back then would shoot six frames a second. However, one shot I will never erase from my mind was this very large hunk of manure flying by the camera lens, frozen in mid air because of the speed the camera was taking pictures. Yes, you know where it landed, dead center in my upper left torso with a splat, missing my face by inches. I wish that had been the only hunk of manure that hit the cameraman and me that day. Everyone had a great laugh, including me and our cameraman after we cleaned ourselves up.

Never get too close to something you know nothing about or you could end up with much worse than egg on your face.

We had other, shall we say, interesting moments producing this program, and it was actually a lot of fun putting it all together. When the program was finished and it worked extremely well for the salespeople, delivering far more total sales within just a few months, the owner decided one day to ask me to work for him as his national sales manager for at least a year.

While I resisted at first, explaining to him over and over that my degree was in broadcasting and audio/visual production, he finally made me an offer I couldn't refuse. Even though it was a career totally out of my field, it ended up being a four and a half year stint allowing me to travel all over this nation, meeting every type of farmer and experiencing every type of farming you can imagine.

It also allowed my wife and I to tour exotic places on sales reward trips like the Bahamas and Europe.

As I mentioned earlier, at the time of negotiating, I had told Bob the owner of the company over and over again, my career was broadcasting and audio/visual production and I was not interested whatsoever. However, being a great salesperson, he refused to accept a no. In fact, he did not even acknowledge my first, second or even third no, and that is a tactic I teach in my sales training seminars to this day. He did not give up easily and he refused to take an absolute no, from a qualified prospect, which I would later learn is the mark of a top 5% salesperson within any sales field.

After a few hours and nearly a fifth of Johnny Walker whiskey between us, he kept upping the offer until it was one I could not refuse (I am sure the booze helped a lot too as he knew it would). It was for one year and I ended up staying in the business for four and a half incredible years. As I said earlier, during that time, I made more money per capita, per year, than I have ever made in my life before or since. As my wife has always said, "I cried when Stan went into the business and I cried when he got out of it."

__Negotiating can be a fascinating part of sales, so make sure when you venture into it, you know what you are doing and your competition doesn't have the upper hand right from the start__. __Obviously, I went to school on this one__.

I gave my two weeks notice at the company where I had produced this program and started getting ready to work with distributors around the country who were selling directly to farmers themselves, along with the salespeople they had working for them. The concept of cutting out the middleman was fantastic and the final price on the farm, regardless of what we were selling, ranged from a little bit less to a lot less than the farmer could buy at his local hardware story.

And remember, in the early 1970's there were no Big Box stores to go to, even if they drove a long way. Sears and Montgomery Wards were about the only big chains they had access to and we could beat those prices hands down, because we bought items by the train carload or semi tractor trailer truck load. In addition, we guaranteed our tools and drill bits unconditionally, just like Craftsman tools, so farmers felt comfortable in dealing with us.

Because I did have some sales experience, the owner of this company decided I only needed a little training in the field, most of which was done in his farmyard selling to me, and then me selling back to him, on the tailgate of his one ton, beautiful, blue and white Chevy pickup truck. He already had a later model ordered just like it so he told me I would be driving this one. It had all the whistles and bells, a powerful 454 engine that got about 8 to 9 miles to the gallon empty or loaded with a few thousand pounds of material, once you got up to 70 miles per hour.

In addition, this truck could do up to 150 miles per hour if you wanted to take the time to wind it out (which I did more than once — but that's later in the book). It also had a CB with a large antenna, dual gas tanks to allow me to go a long way before filling up at around 25 to 35 cents per gallon, and a nice camper topper on the back of the truck bed, with the company's neatly arranged array of nuts and bolts and tools in the back.

If you were really smart, I found out you also carried a cooler in the summer to entice farmers who were busy to "stop for a cool one" because they were so hot and dry. Not wanting to insult the religious types, we would keep the beer in the bottom and if the farmer wanted more than a soda (or pop); you dug down and got him a Bud.

Our main specialty was selling, dycrominated five grade steel nuts and bolts ranging from one-quarter inch, one inch long, up to three quarter and one inch bolts, at least six inches long. They had a gold type look to them with three marks on the head to indicate they were hardened bolts. We also carried Hanson drill bits we replaced for free if they ever broke, as well as ¾-inch socket wrench sets that were unconditionally covered too.

We also had a new nationwide toll free number called a "Watts" line (which was the first 800 numbers). This allowed the farmer to call us anytime for reorders, right from his workshop or from inside his home for free. Bob had a self adhesive sticker to promote this convenience and it was a stroke of genius because if a distributor or salesperson did not call on the farmer when he needed things, he could call us and we would ship them directly to his farm by United Parcel Service, a relatively new company at the time that promised to deliver anywhere the United States Postal office delivered.

Well, it didn't take long before Bob said… "You are as ready as you will ever be. Now you need two weeks of actual experience on the road. Meet me at my house around 6 am this coming Sunday morning. Tell your wife you could be gone as long as up to two weeks and so pack accordingly. I want to end up in Sioux City Iowa no later than nightfall so don't be late."

I thought to myself… 'Why all the way out there? Maybe he planned to train me with all types of farmers and even ranchers, as we sold nuts and bolts and tools across the country.' I didn't give it much thought and when I arrived early at his place that Sunday, we embarked on a beautiful drive across the midsection of our nation's farmland with hardly anything else to see but corn and bean crops the entire way. Bob gave me a quick but thorough education on farming and the "do and don't" on that trip which, helped me immensely later on.

I had noticed the truck was loaded to the hilt with all kinds of products when I arrived so my suitcase joined Bob's on top of everything. Besides the "dos and don'ts" of farming, we were also able to learn a lot more about each other during that drive. We kept a good pace and since we only stopped quickly for food, gas and bodily functions, we arrived at our destination early that evening, and the sun still had a couple of hours before it would set. Bob remarked…. "Man, we made good time." Quite frankly, I was amazed where we ended up and the fact we started in Michigan that morning. We had just put in almost 760 miles of driving!

As we were checking into a motel on the outskirts of town, I heard and saw airplanes taking off and landing more like the volume of a bigger city. Bob commented that this airport some times served as a training airport for takeoffs and landings. Therefore, while Sioux City, Iowa was not that big a town back then, I was seeing both real flights and training ones going on too, and the motel was very close to the airport.

At dinner we began to talk about the schedule of the next day. Suddenly, Bob broke some incredible news to me about as bluntly as he could. "Early tomorrow morning you are going to drive me to the airport because I have an 8 am flight out of here." In shock and thinking, some kind of emergency had come up at home, I

What I Learned In Life From A Liquid Manure Pit

asked. "Anything wrong back home?" His response was nonchalant. "Nope, this will be your indoctrination to all types and kinds of farmers. Your job is to work your way back home stopping on farmers, and selling product to them along the way, *at our list price,* with no discounting. Here's enough cash to more than keep you going in expenses for gas and motels and your goal is to sell out this truck within two weeks! Once you have done that, jump on the closest highway headed East towards Michigan and stop and give me a call along the way when you do."

It is always a good idea to know the sales training program of a company ahead of time so you can get your panic out of the way when you finally hear what it is.

I could not believe my ears! Talk about learning how to swim by being pushed off the end of the dock in deep water. All I could think of as I watched him board that plane that morning was… "You are on your own baby!" and for a moment, panic started to set in. But then a funny thing happened to me. I realized I could do this and the challenge was to do it as well as possible and as soon as possible.

My very first farm was hardly a mile from the airport. I had a road Atlas that showed me I was not that far from Southwestern Minnesota and I was already in Northwestern Iowa, so I decided to head in that direction and start calling on farmers weaving around in that area to get some good experience. I saw crops like Milo and Sunflowers as well as Sorghum and Wheat, along with the usual field corn and beans (all of which I did not realize we grew that much of in this country). Until then, I honestly had no idea there was such a thing as sweet corn and field corn—thank goodness Bob mentioned this to me in our travels to Sioux City.

Well, as I pulled into that first farm, I saw the pickup in the yard (something Bob told me to always look for) and it looked like a decent place. The owner was walking from the house to his big green and white metal pole barn and stopped to watch me driving in. On the side of my truck was the beautiful, oval, red, white and blue Ace Nut & Bolt Company magnetic signs and there was a nice flag on each one too. We greeted and seemed to hit it off rather quickly but I could also see this man's curiosity of who the heck this guy was and what was he selling. That did not take long to answer as

What I Learned In Life From A Liquid Manure Pit

we moved to the back of the truck and I opened it up for him to see all my array of goodies all men love. That's when he noticed the Michigan license plate and said. "You are all the way out here from Michigan selling tools and nuts and bolts?"

__It is usually a good idea to have a good reason for working a long way from home, when you could be working in your own backyard.__

"Yes" I responded as enthusiastically as possible "and you will not believe what our company offers our many farmer and rancher customers around the country." Without hesitating further, I said... "I have a visual program that will tell you exactly what we do and how it will benefit you. May I show it to you?" He was amazed at the television like gadget with no electrical wires and the quality of the pictures and voice once it played. I commented as little as possible as the filmstrip with synchronous voice and music audio presented the company program and the many benefits and advantages to farmers. It was well done if I do say so myself and when it ended, I said (as we trained our salespeople to do), "So what do you think, is this something you would be interested in having on your farm?"

He responded with a buying signal. "It looks good but what's the whole nine yards gonna cost me?" (By the way, this was a term farmers used all the time that I thought had something to do with farming. Later in life I would learn it first was coined in WWI and stood for the length of an ammunition belt for airplanes—so once you shot your whole nine yards, you were in a world of hurt if you were still in a dogfight with an enemy plane).

I had been trained at this point to say... "Well I am glad you asked, that's the best part, and we have an unbelievable price on our lifetime guaranteed drill bit set as well as our 3/4 inch socket set. This bolt set including the short bolt kit and the long bolt kit will only cost you $149.95 (a lot of money back then). Does that sound like something you would be interested in?" I had closed so I knew well enough to shut up and within less than ten seconds of him staring at the two bolt sets, he said. "Yeh, I'll take both sets."

I responded enthusiastically, probably a little more than I should have.... "Great, where do you want me to help you set them up?"

We went into his shop, me carrying the heavy short bolt set and him the long bolt one. Once that was done (and honestly, I was so excited, up until now I had forgotten everything else we sold), I remembered to tell him about the large drill bit set after we walked back to the truck. He wanted that too. Then I showed him the 3/4 socket wrench set and he wanted that too. I left there on cloud nine with a sale of almost $400.00 (the equivalent of well over $1000.00 in today's pricing).

By the end of his drive, in my head, I figured out exactly what one of our salespeople would have made on that sale at 30% (distributors made 40% off the list price and usually paid their salespeople 30%, thus making 10% minimum off of each sale made and up to 40% on items they sold). I also thought to myself.. "Wow, can it be this easy all the time?" Man, even if our guys only closed one out of three sales attempts, they could make some serious money by the end of the week. Well the product and concept was a great idea and so they did make a lot of money.

Later in life, I found myself wondering what would have happened to me if that first sale had not been so perfect and so seemingly easy. I may have gotten down mentally, then portrayed to the next farmer my lack of enthusiasm, and lost sale after sale, simply because I was experiencing a lot of what the all time great motivational speaker and salesperson, Zig Ziglar always called "stinking—thinking".

Well, I have to tell you, while I certainly did not do that well with each call, I seemed to always sell them something, even if it was a small tool, an easy out set or the drill bits. However, everything I sold made the truck that much lighter and got me closer to my goal of being able to turn that truck East and head home.

At the end of the day I did a thorough inventory check of what was on the truck based on what Bob had told me was there at the start, and I looked at my day's total sales. I figured I could easily hit my needed goal of selling out the truck within two weeks or less. So then, I carefully figured out how much more I would have to sell each day on average to reach that goal sooner. I wrote it down and placed it in the cab of the truck to look at all the time.

To be a top producer in sales, you must have specific daily, weekly, monthly and yearly goals that are reasonable to obtain, yet

large enough to stretch you. In addition, you should review them constantly to stay on track.

I wanted to get as much experience with different types of farmers (and their farms) as possible. I also wanted to hit as many states as possible in this upcoming two-week span. For this reason, I developed a kind of meandering but planned route that would take me across southern Minnesota, drop me down into Iowa heading back West for a while, then dip into Missouri, my home state, and then swing up into Illinois, hoping to wrap things up in one and a half to two weeks.

Therefore, I must admit I kind of "cherry picked" the best looking farms and I would drive twenty to fifty miles sometimes before stopping again. I used secondary highways to travel and stop at farms either just off of them, or a mile or two away, while not getting on a superhighway until towards the end of my entire journey. I was having a great time and the farmers were buying because it was a good year. Crops were in and cultivated for the most part, and everyone was kind of waiting for the fall harvest down the road.

In other words, I had a great product, a great new kind of on-the-farm service and I was hitting farmers at the right time of year with this program. I was smart enough to know my success was not necessarily my super sales expertise, but things were clicking and I made the most of it.

On my third day out, I was moving across South Central Minnesota when I was closing in on a nice looking farm. However, a storm was blowing in and it was very ugly looking. In fact, it looked so dark and ugly, I was scanning the sky for a funnel cloud. I pulled into the farm as the storm was approaching. About then the strong gusts of wind ahead of the storm arrived and the dust made it extremely difficult to see.

I saw the owner of the farm looking off to the Southwest and he never heard me pull in his yard. I shouted to him over the noise being made by the blowing wind and he turned to see me. He was a little surprised and then he said… "You might want to drive that fancy pickup truck of yours into my shed. That's hail coming damn it all," as he pointed to a greenish looking monster cloud… "and it could be large." I swung around and backed into his barn just in time

What I Learned In Life From A Liquid Manure Pit

to have the rain arrive in torrents along with even heavier gusts of wind.

His pickup truck was already in the shed. I found out later his wife was in town so he and I just watched mother nature unfold. At one point he told me if a funnel cloud appeared his tornado shelter was by the back door (as he pointed to it). I wondered why he and I were not in it already when suddenly the hail began to fall and it was awful. It was golf ball in size to start and grew to nearly baseball size in just a few moments. He started swearing terribly and I was so glad my truck was in his pole barn.

In my lifetime, I had never seen hail like this before nor since, and it really scared me, especially because of the awful sound of this hail hitting his metal pole barn roof and house. It came down with a horrible racket and seemed to last forever as it piled up in his farmyard a few inches deep. He had some livestock in a field nearby and I could see them being pelted mercilessly. I half expected some of them to be killed. He said a few more cuss words I could hardly hear over the racket. At the time, I assumed I knew the reason for him doing so, but I did not yet know the real reason because I was still so new to the farming game.

After the hail moved on and even before the rain stopped, he continued to cuss loudly as he walked to the edge of a nearby cornfield. I followed close behind him nearly slipping and falling on the piled up hail. Then, for the first time, I knew exactly what he had been so upset about when the hail was hammering us. The standing corn had been stripped to shreds and it was destroyed for the most part.

I could not believe what had happened and in such a short time. He then said…. "I am sure it got all my other crops too, especially my wheat field I was going to harvest in a few days." I realized then and now, he was not going to be interested in talking to me about nuts and bolts and tools. In fact, when he finally asked me who I was, I told him and he said…. "I am not in any mood to talk to a salesperson right now! Sorry." I said I was sorry too and asked if I could help and he said…. "Yeh, get that four hundred acres of corn back for me will yah!" Needless to say, I left quickly after that. I do not know how much he lost in crops that day but it did make me realize for the first time in my life how vulnerable farmers where to weather conditions.

When the sales environment is perfect, keep on selling as long as you can because things can change quickly, and sometimes very quickly, to shut it down altogether, or at the least, slow it down significantly.

I moved on and tried to find areas where that storm and hail had missed and amazingly enough, it did not take long. It was as if that storm came through in pockets of hail. Most of the farms ten miles further down the road got much needed rain without hail and I even saw a rainbow, which almost seemed to point me in the right direction. I continued to work my way East across Southern Minnesota, looking for the "low hanging fruit" while "cherry picking as I went".

Then something happened to me, which was my first unforgettable story in this business, and one of the most remarkable ones too. I was somewhere around fifteen to twenty miles or so outside of Mankato Minnesota (which was a much smaller city thirty some years ago, than it is now) when I spied a beautiful farm, with a few big, shiny, metal grain bins, a nice home and a large green and white pole barn along with some adjoining buildings. In addition, I had begun to learn how to recognize seed corn farmers because they would have various signs near the road promoting a particular hybrid or variety of field corn.

These signs would be at the end of neatly cut open sections of corn crops, identified by a sign stating the particular hybrid of seed corn. In this way, farmers passing by could get out of their pickup and take a close up look at the different crops, in various stages of growth until harvest. Over the next four and a half years, I would come to know just about every brand of field corn out there including some that were homegrown. These homegrown brands were usually sold in just a few surrounding counties.

Well, I pulled into the yard and there wasn't a pickup truck anywhere to be seen. I got out, slammed the door of my truck and was headed to the backdoor of the house when a woman came running out to me from the barn and said... "Oh thank goodness, I could sure use your help." Now I have to tell you, while I had a

What I Learned In Life From A Liquid Manure Pit

Michigan license plate, by day two of my venture, I had bought a pair of nice leather cowboy boots and a cowboy hat for my attire so as to develop my persona (I devote a chapter to this persona thing later). It worked for me the entire four and a half years I sold to farmers across the country. People talked about the nut and bolt salesman with the cowboy hat all the time. So when the lady of the farm saw me in this getup, there was no doubt in her mind I could handle what I was about to get involved in because she was sure I had been confronted with the situation before, and had plenty of experience. *Boy, I quickly discovered she was wrong!*

Not knowing what it was she wanted of me, as we hurried back into the barn, I began to get some hints. She was saying things like… "I got a calf that isn't dropping right. It's coming out breech. My husband is gone and the Vet cannot get here for another hour or more." She also said something like… "I can't get my hands on her legs good enough, and I am not strong enough to turn the calf or pull it out with these pulling ropes." By then I saw this cow (to this day, I clearly remember this big ole cow, restrained somewhat, but laying on the ground looking at me and with her big ole eyes staring at me, and her private parts dilated). She was definitely in pain and mooing a lot (actually it was more like moaning I think) as she continued to go through contractions. A shot of adrenalin rushed through me as I realized for the first time what this lady wanted me to do! I had not been born on a farm of course, but I knew what a breech birth was in humans and how dangerous it was to both the mother and the baby. Both could die if something wasn't done quickly.

In an instant, this lady was helping me take my shirt off and wash up in a bucket of what looked like soapy water. Next, she offered me what I think was a petroleum jelly or cream or something to rub on my arms. It was then I realized I was about to insert my arms into that cow's dilated uterus! I also realized I was supposed to somehow loop or tie a rope around the calf's feet, and in the meantime, try to turn that calf enough so I could pull it out with my hands or the rope. I learned weeks later *after* all this took place that I was missing about 95% of the information I needed to have been performing this vital function. 'You've got to be kidding me?!'…. I thought to myself. Bob never warned me about this. Where in the heck was he when I needed him the most? This too was not in the training manual. Well, at least not yet.

I had only played a cowboy on TV so far, and in farm sales, I had only been playing one for a few days, so I just did what I thought I was supposed to do, never realizing how complicated this breech birth thing is and all the proper steps a veterinarian would be taking about now. I began inserting first my hands and then my arms, slowly into that mother cow's business end. She turned and looked at me and mooed so loud, I nearly jumped right out of there in total fright, but I kept going while this farmer's wife gave both me and the cow encouragement (the cow had a name the lady kept saying to her, but for the life of me, I do not remember it—Susie maybe?).

I do remember starting to get my hands on that calf's legs and I also could feel its rear end. Now, using common sense, I was trying to think how I was going to pull it out of there and what I should do next. I moved its legs around some trying to get a good grip, and with my feet somehow braced, I started pulling with all my might, totally forgetting to use the pulling ropes. All of a sudden, probably in sheer fright of this weirdo city guy with his arms up her privates, combined with my pulling, this cow somehow dilated a bunch more and pushed very hard at the same time. The result after a few moments was a calf and a little bit of afterbirth in my lap. Wow, what an incredible experience! I could now add this to my resume along with me watching one of my Elkhound dogs deliver pups at 3 am in the morning.

It is said in life that those who show up, run the world. In addition, it is also said, sometimes you can find yourself in the right place, at the right time. **When both happen to you, you could be headed for an even better experience later on.**

Basically, I had not done a whole lot except show up and be at the right place, at the right time. Frankly though, I think I must have scared that cow so bad, she dropped that calf in a New York minute. This lady did not see what actually happened, all she saw was the result and she instantly started praising me while talking to the cow at the same time.

As she helped me clean up, I actually enjoyed observing my first close up birth involving a large animal. And hey, I had played a part in the delivery of that cute but still wet calf. The lady placed the calf near the mother's head and she began licking the calf to dry her off (something else very important I learned that day that mother cattle must do to their calves, especially if they are born out in the open in cold weather, to keep them from getting sick and dying of pneumonia). As we relaxed some, this lady kept tending to the cow and calf but she began asking me about who I was and what I was doing (seed corn farmers get a lot of drop ins so it was normal for me to have stopped anyway). I told her briefly who I was and what I was doing. "Well, my husband will not be home until later this afternoon. He will want to thank you for this. Are you staying in Mankato tonight or are you headed further on?"

Actually, I had planned to stay in Mankato, so I gave her an affirmative and she responded. She knew about the only motel on this side of town and then said.. "Great, please call us early this evening, I'll give you our phone number if you have something to write it on. I am sure he will want to see what you have, especially after you saved the day and all."

In sales, as in life, you have to capitalize on these types of 'manna from heaven' windfalls and so I told her I most surely would call him tonight.

I hit one more farm towards Mankato, shared the experience with that farmer as though I were a veteran at doing this thing, and sold a few things to him, but nothing spectacular. I hit town and found that motel, freshened up a bit, grabbed a light dinner and made the phone call. Mr. seed corn farmer answered and he told me to most definitely to "come back out here as soon as you can". Rain was coming in again from the Southwest and it really started to come down hard when I finally arrived at his place. Plus, it was pitch black out now. I noticed a lot of pickups parked around the yard. Thank goodness there was no hail in this storm or a lot of nice pickup trucks would have been damaged. I could see a good size opening of the two large sliding doors in his pole barn and lots of light pouring out from it. I even thought I saw some smoke coming out of the crack between the doors.

Suddenly I saw a good-sized man wearing a seed corn hat, opening the doors wider despite the driving rain and he seemed to be signaling me to turn around and back into the pole barn. It was a bit hard to see in my mirrors but as I got closer, and began backing further into the barn, I saw a lot more farmers. I also noticed a large barbeque pit going with something big turning on it. Well, what I had been invited to was a seed corn party with a pig roast and all the sweet corn on the cob and extra food you could eat.

This farmer shook my hand and thanked me for what I had done earlier that day, and shouted and told everybody "this is the guy who helped my wife save my cow and calf today." He then said… "So show me what you've got." The rest is history and a great sales lesson. He bought one of everything and told everybody to come over and "see if they were interested in anything."

Windfalls in sales and sheer luck are going to happen to you if you keep on making the calls and showing up. And sometimes they will be incredible ones.

Wow, I could not write the orders up fast enough. By the time I was done, I had sold well over $2000.00 at one stop! As I drove back to the motel later that night, it suddenly dawned on me I had taken a giant step towards my goal of being empty and going home. I began to realize a few remarkable things had taken place too.

First, even though I had no idea what I was doing early that day, I had performed an act of kindness with no hidden agendas and I was rewarded freely and handsomely for it. Second, once you get an influential person to buy from you, a "bandwagon effect" takes place as others want to do what that top, respected person did (we call it a bandwagon effect in sales because everyone wants to get on the bandwagon in the parade). Third, for years afterwards, this farmer and his friends would be a wonderful referral base for us in that area, so when a distributor took over that area, he would be smart to take good care of them to maintain their loyalty. Finally, if you really have a great product and you can get it to the right people, sometimes all at the same time, a feeding frenzy can take place.

The next day I was still on my own, but as I headed out for my first call, I remembered the shirt pocket bandwagon idea Bob had shared with me on our drive to Sioux City. Since I wanted to head back West and drop down into Iowa and eventually my home state of Missouri, I could see these farmers who bought from me had city addresses that covered a decent area spread out in all directions. So, as Bob had suggested when you have a lot of sales, I stuffed all those invoices in my shirt pocket and made my first stop. I had so many in my pocket, it was almost ripping the seams. In addition, I could see the eyes of the farmer I stopped at first, looking directly at my pocket with great curiosity.

"Well, it looks like you have been selling a lot of stuff to my neighbors. Mind if I find out who they are and what they bought?" Keep in mind here, he had not even looked at what I was selling yet. I responded by pulling them out of my pocket and darn if he didn't know em all, even though some of them lived miles away (I learned that day too you may live one place but to have a lot of acreage, you sometimes have to farm all over). He then said… "So what yah got?"

That's all it took and soon, another sale was made without much effort. And like the night before, I did not have to use the A/V program. I was using the sales template I had actually helped write for the audio-visual program so it was already ingrained in my mind. In addition, I remembered that tactic (i.e. the invoices in the shirt pocket). It turned out later this pocket stuffed with invoices tactic worked so well, I decided to teach it to everyone who worked for us for the remaining time I was the national sales manager. I found out later some guys embellished this tactic by purposely ripping their pockets a little, just so they could get more invoices stuffed in there.

Being creative in sales is a critical success factor and you need to always be challenging yourself on ways to do things better. And as I said before, when you are hot, don't stop until you absolutely have to!

Eventually, because of that giant, multiple sale, within a few more days, the truck was nearly empty. So now, to try and speed things up, when I stopped at a farm, I used the adapted sales line I learned as a high school, door-to-door salesperson. I would weave into my pitch that… "I'm working my way home and as soon as the truck is empty, I get to hit highway 80 and head East."

I never got to Missouri, my home state, on that first trip because I could see I was going to sell out and it would only lengthen my time to accomplish my goal. I was now somewhere around Davenport Iowa and ready to head towards highway 80 within a day at the most. Early the next day, what I was sure would be my last stop, I pulled into a very nice looking farm owned by an older farmer. Unfortunately, while he showed interest in everything I had, I spent two hours showing him all of it and getting more and more frustrated by the moment, because I was so close to being empty. But darn it all, he just would not buy anything.

When it was all said and done, after what seemed about forty closes on my part to ask him to buy something, this guy didn't even buy a $4.95 easy out set. As I pulled out of his farm, I was mad at myself for wasting my time. And since his farm was on a small rise, I immediately starting looking around for another farm and spotted a nice looking one a section (or mile) away to the south. When I reached it, I caught the owner and to my amazement, the sale was culminated in less than 30 minutes, and it was a handsome one too! Basically, that sale cleaned me out. After writing up the sale and getting my check, I asked him if he knew the farmer a mile over (and I pointed to his farm)? He smiled a big ole grin and said.. "Yeah, why do you ask?"

I had to be careful because Bob had warned me, most of the time in a farming community, many people are related and they definitely know each other very well. So I said… "Well, I just spent two hours talking to him showing him everything I had and he loved it all, but when it came to buying, he didn't even buy a $5 easy out set. Now I drive down here to your farm, and you also saw the value in what I have to offer, but you bought just about everything in (I looked at my watch) thirty minutes. Any ideas why?"

He laughed and said… "He's a nice guy and a good farmer, but he's also a cob roller." I said… "A what?" He said it again… "A cob roller. Here let me show you what I mean." We walked over to an open-air corncrib (used to feed his hogs) and he pulled a full ear of field corn out of it and laid it on the ground. He took a stick nearby and said… "Now watch this." He began to nudge the ear of corn. It was slightly tapered so it began to go in a wide circle. Eventually it ended up back where it started from having gone in a complete circle. "You see what happened there?"

What I Learned In Life From A Liquid Manure Pit

"Yeah, I guess so." I answered, "The corn cob did a complete circle." He then said... "Right..., he loves to talk to people and he is very friendly, but he hardly ever buys things without thinking about it for a long time. He is what we call in these parts a 'cob roller' and you were the stick. And you know what, he enjoyed every minute of it. He figures if he really wants it, and you really want the sale bad enough, you will call on him again and maybe get the sale, and then again, maybe not."

Well to this day, I now know when I am dealing with a 'cob roller' and when I am dealing with someone who is ready to take action. After that stop, I did not have any more short nut and bolt kits to sell and I had a couple of long bolt kits. In addition to that, there was very little of anything else left on my truck and I had run out of drill bits a long time ago. I stopped in a local town and called Bob, and told him what I had left and should I sell that too or pack it in and head to Michigan. It was exactly nine days from when we parted in Sioux City and I did not work on Sunday.

"Bring it on home, you have done great! You sure you didn't discount?" I told him it had all been sold at retail off the price list he gave me and he said... "Well that's fantastic. That's our new price list I expect you to release when you get back here and you will be proof to the distributors and their salespeople that what we have to sell is not based on price like they think it is."

Later on with his company, I would find this to be very true again and again. We were selling the features, advantages, benefits, and *value added* concepts of our program, not less expensive nuts, bolts and tools (which was an advantage of course). Well, it did not take me long to figure out the quickest way home and I hit the Michigan state line late that evening riding on cloud nine. I had thousands of dollars in checks and cash on me and for four and a half years, this became a normal, everyday occurrence.

Professional selling tactics are the same in any industry so once you learn them and utilize them consistently, you will have a great job for life, regardless of what you are selling. The number one rule though is to discipline yourself to learn them and then to use those tactics consistently and congruently.

Chapter 2.

It's No Bull Selling To Farmers And It Can Be A Risky Business Too

The American farm is one of the most dangerous places to work if you are not careful and even then, it's an OSHA nightmare. There are lots of things that can grab you and tear an arm off before you can blink your eye; there are animals that can get out of control and hurt you bad or even kill you; there are chemicals you need to be very careful with as you handle them; there is equipment that in one second can go from being your best, most efficient farming friend, to your worst enemy. And that's just for starters.

I first discovered this while producing the sales program for the Ace Bolt and Nut Company. The crew had finished shooting in one area of the farm and they were headed to the next staging area. I had stayed behind for a few moments while reviewing my notes, my script and my shot sheet on my clipboard. When I finally looked up,

What I Learned In Life From A Liquid Manure Pit

I had not seen how everyone had gotten to where they were when I came out of the barn we last shot in, so I began to look around.

I saw them about a couple hundred feet away near a silo. Since I had not seen what route they took to get there, I began walking through a sort of short space that was wide at one end and narrow at the other, with the barn wall on one side and a bunch of cattle on the other side of a metal type fence. Well, something I did or some smell I gave off spooked them and the next thing you know, that fence had me penned to the outside barn wall and I thought I would be crushed. Then, as quick as it happened, it was over and I was too embarrassed to let anyone know my stupidity when I joined up with the group. What could have been a quick disaster turned out to be some sore ribs later that night. However, as I learned over and over again, that is how quick things can go wrong on a farm, especially if you are not careful and stay alert at all times. Apparently I had walked through a kind of portable fence that was used to single out cattle for various purposes.

Well, being as I was on a fast learning curve in this "selling to the farmer" business, I was destined to make a lot of mistakes like that one and hopefully live to tell about them. To help pay for my sales manager position, when I traveled between distributorships, I would sell in areas not yet covered by a distributor. The funds I made not only helped pay my way, but it helped pay for a number of other marketing things too. Therefore, not two weeks after I was back out in the field moving from one distributor to another, I came across a nice farm that had been purposely built on a rise so you could see crops and farmland in all directions. There wasn't a pickup in the yard so as I glanced around that 360-degree view. That is when I saw a tractor cultivating what I would later recognize as some late-planted soybeans (some farmers called it plowing) in a large field to my West.

Between me and the farmer was a small field or pasture and it looked like there were a couple of light, tan colored cows in the north corner. I could not see from my vantage point how to get to this farmer except by walking across this field not more than a hundred yards wide and maybe 200 yards long. I could see eventually he would come to the small field fence directly across from me, and then turn around, and head back the other way again. With that in mind, I figured if I timed my walk across that field to his arrival at the end row where he would turn around, then I could tell him who I was and find out how I could get to him and show him my wares.

About that time, the wife came out of the house and asked if I was looking for her husband. I introduced myself and I said,... "I sure am mam. Would that happen to be him over in that bean field cultivating?" She answered affirmatively and proceeded to turn around and go back into the house before I could ask her how I could get to her husband. I figured it was probably so obvious, she didn't bother telling me.

Cardinal rule here in life; always take the time to get good directions, especially when you are selling in farming country because your life could depend upon it. Especially if you are still on a severe learning curve.

Well, he was closer to the end row now and it wasn't that far across the field. And if I didn't get a move on, I might miss him. Plus, those cows, even though I was going to cross about in the middle of the field, were at the other end of the field. I was not smart enough to be afraid of them. So I got some gloves from my truck that I figured I could protect myself from the barbed wire. Then I walked to the barbed wire fence near a post, and was about to climb over it when I realized the top wire, which had no barbed wire, was very thin and I feared I might break it if I stepped on it, climbing over the fence like I normally did. I had not seen this before so I went to plan "B" and carefully made a gap between the lower strands of wire with one boot on the bottom strand of wire, and my hands on the second strand of bob-wire. Then I stepped through holding one wire up and the other one down, being careful not to catch my clothes on the barbed wire. Then I proceeded to walk across the field.

It was almost exactly at this point the farmer noticed me and waved. I waved back and proceeded to continue strolling across the field, avoiding cow pies along the way. I never once glanced at the cows at the other end of the field. Next thing I know he waved at me with both hands and jumped off his tractor shouting something. Then he seemed to be pointing to the cows so I turned and was shocked to see one was galloping towards me, and I thought I could

What I Learned In Life From A Liquid Manure Pit

see horns too. Whoa Nelly, something is definitely wrong with this picture! In addition, even at a distance this dude was a big hunker.

I could hear the farmer shouting to me plainly now.... "Good God man, hurry. Run and get over here before he kills you!" Hey, city boy or not, when you hear those kinds of words, you need to kick it in to action. All I could think of was 'feet don't fail me now' and I was running as hard as I had run since my high school track meet days. Well okay, maybe not quite that fast but at least it felt like I was. The adrenaline was pumping big time now.

Next, this farmer did a wild thing. He placed one boot on the lowest strand of barbed wire and held the second one up with his two bare hands. It did not take a rocket scientist to figure out instantly what he wanted me to do. And with twenty feet to go I could hear that bull's hoofs galloping fast and I heard him breathing hard and bearing down on me. With no time to spare, I dove through the opening almost perfectly with only one nasty little scratch and torn spot in my Levi jeans to show for it. The bull pulled up short of the barbed wire fence he knew very well, but he was really ticked off at me and hung around for a while, with those big eyes glaring at me and snorting.

This farmer was beside himself. He shouted... "Good grief man, you could have been killed! That Charolais bull could have bowled you over and killed you before I could get to you. What the hell were you thinking?" Well, once again, I had experienced something I will never forget and I lived to tell about it too, *thank you Lord*. However, I had to come up with something to explain why I did what I did so I blurted out something like... "I was so intent on coming over to see you, I did not see him." Still shouting, he exclaimed... "You cannot make those kinds of mistakes around any bull, especially this one. He's a prize one and about as large as he will ever get. He's a mean one too. You just walked through his pasture." The bull was just beginning to walk away but he was still staring at me with those big eyes.

For some reason, that's when I also realized there was a ring in that bull's nose. At the time, I did not know why but I later found out this helps control them when you want to move them (another new thing to learn). It is in a very tender part of their nose and they have

What I Learned In Life From A Liquid Manure Pit

been trained very early that if they followed the person holding the ring, (which actually is tied into a halter because holding that ring directly was not a good idea), and did not give them trouble, it did not hurt them.. I must admit I never saw it done but that's what I was told, so I believed it to be true.

Then I also noticed that thin wire again strung above the top of all the barbed wire. But this time I also noticed some white, glass type things holding the wire between the fence posts, which somehow, I had totally missed earlier (hey, I was still learning, remember?). Apparently this farmer had taken all the precautions to keep that big fellow in that field by having an electric wire on the top of all that barbed wire so his prize bull would not be giving away his champion lines for free by jumping over that fence. I found out later on in our conversation, he did all his mating with that bull in that one field I had so stupidly entered. Good grief I thought, it was his bedroom I had invaded!

Somehow, he bought the fact that I was not a total idiot (which I was convinced I was by now). Instead, he came to the conclusion that I was somewhat fearless and had just made a stupid mistake, even if it did almost cost me my life. Eventually we got around to why I had made this dangerous venture across that mating field to reach him and he said… "You know, if you had asked my wife, she could have told you how easy it is to come around to where I have a gate and my pickup truck parked. Wasn't she up at the house?" I assured him she was, and I had talked to her, but I failed to ask her how to reach him. So I told him I took the shortest trip between two points across the field.

After a short exchange, there was no choice about crossing the field back again of course, so I hitched a ride with him, standing on the side of the tractor, all the way to the other half section of the field, cultivating beans all along the way. We got to talking and soon we had built some rapport. Then we walked over to his pickup truck and we drove back to the house so he could see what I had. More than once he brought up the narrow escape again as we drove back to his house. I just kept smiling and keeping with my story of poor misjudgment.

After a good hour, he bought just about everything we offered. Normally farmers carry a checkbook on them but this time he had left his in the house. As we walked in the kitchen, he told his wife about what just happened. She stared at me with an unbelievable look because she now realized, when she last saw me last, I headed out across the field instead of driving around to see her husband. She never noticed my pickup truck was still out by the equipment shed.

In those days, people were so trusting in farm country and maybe they still are today. She had briefly talked to me, saw the sign on the side of my truck and my persona of looking like a cowboy, and then never gave it another thought until now. As I drove out of their driveway, I was able to drive by those Charolais cattle again and take a closer look. Yep, you guessed it, that bull was trying to do his duty with one of those cows. All I could think of was how lucky I had really been that day.

<u>No bull, if you want to survive in sales and live to tell about it, you need to know a lot more information than just your sales pitch.</u>

Chapter 3.

Prosperous Cold Calls On Farmers You Just Met For The First Time

—∽—

Most salespeople dread cold calls. The basic reasons are simple: (1) you don't have much, if any idea how things will go (2) you will probably not be as prepared as you could have been IF you had done some research ahead of time (3) cold calls run a very high rate of rejection and therefore, usually a low rate of closing (4) it scares the heck out of most salespeople and (5) there isn't much money in it for most salespeople because they have all the above working against them, they are mentally whipped before they start, and they lack the courage and fortitude to learn how to do it right.

Selling door to door as I did in a college summer job for Fuller Brush and selling farm to farm as I did in this industry, was 90% cold calls back in those days. In both cases, you made the calls, and you followed a sales system or template that could instantly be customized to the person you were selling to and the environment you were selling in at the time. You mirrored and adjusted quickly to the personalities you were dealing with and as you followed that proven template, you usually had an incredibly high closing ratio, especially when you were great at what you were doing and enjoyed doing it too. Then, when you add the incredible power of enthusiasm, you have a winning sales combination.

__Enthusiasm in sales and in life is an absolute, critical success factor. I have seen many new salespeople set records in companies with little more than enthusiasm going for them. I also found the biggest killer of enthusiasm was getting around the old timers who tried to get you back to reality and down to their non-enthusiastic level.__

In the previous two chapters, I discussed cold calls on farmers somewhat but now I would like to share some specific things I learned during those four and a half years that made these cold calls, and those I would make many years later in other sales capacities, extremely successful and a heck of a lot easier while being a lot of fun too.

There were some obvious signs to notice when you drove into a farmer's place. You took note of their tractors and combines, the size and condition of their pole barn and (where they kept their equipment) other buildings, silos (types and the total number), various implements in the yard (things attached to tractors and combines to perform various functions), livestock, the condition of their home and the overall condition and neatness of the place. Combined, this would give you some idea of who you were about to call on, but you still had to meet them face to face to really size up the situation.

This proved especially true if you ran across a farmer away from his farm, tending to his crops or working on his equipment at a remote staging location. In this business, this happened more often than not. In fact, because farmers in those days and even more so today, had to buy and lease land wherever they could, I would run across farmers up to five, ten and even as much as fifteen miles from their main farm. Today, with the cost of fuel, I would expect that is not as practical anymore unless you are a corporate farm.

Besides discussing many other cold call experiences in other chapters of my book, here are some other interesting examples of cold calls that still flashback to me now and then because of their uniqueness. In one instance, I had just driven into a yard and saw a pickup truck. My normal practice was to then turn my truck sideways to a farmers shed, getting ready to back into the shade and out of the hot sun while I pitched him. Not five seconds more and here comes the farmer madder than a wet hen, holding a ¾ inch socket wrench, with a broken handle. I remembered how Bob had taught me in the training not to try and negotiate at this time, when you ran up against an unhappy customer. Instead, you needed to "Instantly neutralize the situation and then ask them to buy other things you had, once they were calmed down."

    I jumped out of the truck and went to the back of it, opened the door to my camper/topper and pulled out a brand new socket set as the farmer caught up with me. I handed him a new wrench and took the broken one out of his hands and asked… "You are all set, no charge. Are all the sockets still in good shape?" He was speechless and things went very well from that point on. He had been disarmed instantly and had no reason to complain anymore. By the way, back then we replaced tools free like Sears did, even if we saw evidence of marks on the ¾-inch socket set handle. Those marks almost always came from what farmers call a "cheater bar", which is a six to eight foot long hollow pipe. They used it to get lots of extra leverage by placing it on the handle of the wrench, and then jumping on it. Even then, we still honored the breakage and replaced it free!

Anytime you are confronted with a customer service situation that is going to be heated, if not addressed immediately, assure them you will handle it as quickly as possible and move on with the sales encounter.

    Another time I was traveling across Illinois to Southern Indiana to meet up with a distributor. As I mentioned before, as the national sales manager of the company, to help offset my traveling costs, the company kept the cost of the materials sold off my truck, plus most of the 40% discount given off the list price to the distributors. Besides my salary, I would be allowed to keep a certain amount of each sale, to give me incentive to make the stop and make the sales. Driving across country between territories allowed me to kind of "cherry pick the low hanging fruit" and hit the obvious good prospects while driving by the questionable ones.

One day I pulled into a farm where a young, beefy farmer was working on his big Massy Ferguson tractor. He had a hat on that said… "I hate green!" He has a shirt on that said…. "I eat John Deere Tractors for Lunch!" (this meant for you readers who have never been exposed to this kind of thing that he was involved in tractor pulls in a big way and loved beating John Deere pullers in a big way.) He took one look at me and exclaimed with some foul language sprinkled in…. "Well now, ain't you and your truck a pretty picture to lay eyes upon?" I smiled, introduced myself, and then tried to get him talking about himself and what he was doing.

<u>Never take the bait to talk about yourself first in a sales encounter. You need to get the customer talking about the most important person they know, themselves, and find out their interest. I also get their name quickly and use it often from then on in the sales encounter because our name is one of the sweetest words we ever here each day.</u>

He showed me some new, high powered adjustments he was making and said if I wanted to wait a few moments, he was going to "fire this baby up and see how it's running with these new carburetors." I was ahead of schedule and only needed to get to Evansville Indiana by nightfall. I watched him work and never said anything about what I was doing until he finally asked, while still working on tightening a bolt…. "So what the heck is Ace Nut and Bolt anyway?" There was my opening so I said…. "Hey, finish up first and then I'll show you. By the way, I have a cooler in the back with a cold one for you too, when you get ready." With the temperature in the low 90's that day, he suddenly stopped what he was doing and said… "Well, this can wait if you've got a cold one." And he proceeded to walk to the back of the truck where I opened it up and found him an ice, cold beer. He gulped the beer half way down and then said… "What yah got in there?"

The rest of the story is that while he already had most of the tools I carried, he did not have a decent drill bit set (he was missing a lot of them due to breakage) and he did not have any organized nut and bolt collection. He bought our short bolt and long bolt set. It

What I Learned In Life From A Liquid Manure Pit

was a great sale. Afterwards I asked… "So how much longer before you finish up so I can hear what this baby sounds like and see it in action?" He said… "You really want to do that? I will need to get you some ear plugs?" I responded… "Sure!" and he proceeded to tell me he would be ready to fire it up in about five to ten minutes. "Great" I said, "show me where you want your nut and bolt sets placed and I will do that while you keep working."

He did, I did, and soon I was witnessing my first close up of a high powered, extremely modified and powerful tractor. I had to put my fingers in my ears because he forgot to get me those earplugs and it actually hurt my ears as he revved her up. It was an incredible sight and sound to behold as he tore up some ground in front of me as he revved it up in spurts. As far as I could tell, those new carburetors must have been working quite well and he had a big smile on his face to verify that as he shut her down.

Time and time again I learned that in sales, building rapport with potential customers is a critical step. If you show sincere interest in people and can get people talking about what interests them, while allowing them to know you care about them, more than you care about making a sale (and you don't try to rush the sale), they will open up to you, and buy much more from you.

Well now, while I had never seen a tractor pull "live", within two hours, I knew everything there was to know about the sport (or at least I thought so). It was fascinating to think that these guys in various classes of tractors, would pull a weighted sled across a clay bed track with weights that kept shifting automatically as the sled moved, making the sled more and more difficult to pull. In the meantime, those babies belched smoke and fire and tore eardrums up, but the crowd loved every minute of it. (I have a brother-in-law who is a farmer and he went to many of these events. He is extremely hard of hearing and I sometimes wonder if these big ole, loud tractors hadn't exacerbated his problem over the years.)

The neat thing about this guy was that after he bought from me, he had a buddy he wanted me to go see a few miles away. I was already running late now and this was the day before cell phones. In addition, CB radios were only good for short distances of up to ten miles on a good day. However, I also knew another cardinal rule in sales was to never let a referral or "bird in the hand" get away from you.

When a satisfied customer wants to take you to a potential customer to act as a reference for you, do not hesitate because these third party sales are the easiest to make and best of all, 9 times out of 10 they will close. Plus, you will find that you will sell them more than you normally would.

He led the way and we drove over to his buddy's farm. Now here is what he said almost verbatim when we got out of the truck and I shook this guys hand... "You gotta take a look at this guy's nut and bolt kits and he has some drill bits he replaces for free when you break them, honest." His buddy came to the back of the truck and whether it was friend pressure or peer pressure, it didn't matter. I had another good sale in moments and I was sure I would be able to put the hammer down and make some time up. Well not so fast, this guy was a tractor puller too and he had another Massey monster. You guessed it, they wanted me to listen to this one and see it perform a bit too.

Oh well, the company made a lot of money on these two calls and I only lost ten percent of my hearing permanently in the process. In addition, I could make a call in the next town and let the distributor know I would be an hour late or so. And I made two new friends for the company in the process. I saw them at the Farm Machinery show six months later and they told me a lot of guys around their place wanted our stuff so I figure those two stops eventually netted both the company and me a ton of money.

Never rush a sale when the customer is buying because as the ole saying goes... "A bird in the hand is worth two in the bush" and those two can lead to many more sales now and/or later.

Chapter 4.

A Father and Son Farming Team Teach Me a Lesson I Will Never Forget

—ᵥᵥᵥ—

Once again, I was headed across country between distributors going down a two-lane road in the middle of nowhere (which was actually somewhere in North Central Illinois). I was doing my usual "cherry picking" between distributors territories and spied a nice farm on each side of the road. They looked like twins except for one thing. The one to the South was a much newer home. However, I did not see a pickup truck in that yard so I glanced at the farm to the North and spied two of them.

As I pulled in, I laughed because now that I was a veteran at this, I drove past a sign, which read… "Absolutely no salesmen." Another one below that read… "We shoot every third salesman that dares to stop here, and the second one just left." This stops amateurs

What I Learned In Life From A Liquid Manure Pit

dead in their tracks, but not us pros, because we knew their bark was never that bad. Actually, these farmers were usually an easy touch for salesmen so they put those signs up to keep most of them away and keep themselves from being tempted. Well, I found out a short time later that those signs on this particular farm really were intended to keep salesmen away. Let me explain why.

As I drove into the yard, I saw an older gentlemen farmer and a guy in his late twenties or early thirties. They were working on a very large, twelve row John Deere combine and stopped and looked up when I pulled in. It was obvious from the start the older guy felt like I was an interruption but I soon found out the younger one was interested in what I had to say. He followed me to the back of my pick up truck and the older gentlemen, who I found out quickly was his father, kind of came over and watched, but stayed back a good ten to fifteen feet being very noncommittal. So while I tried to include him now and then in the conversation, he just would not engage. Meanwhile, his son was eating up everything I showed him.

Buying signals were all over this guy and eventually he motioned to his dad to come over and take a closer look. The father grumbled and said a few things. I acted as if I did not hear what he was saying including his questioning of my birthrights. I could sense the tension rising as the son tried a second time to get the father to "take a look". The dad seemed to be in good health and good shape, as did his son. Frankly, I was glad one of them liked me. Then something strange happened. The son said a few cuss words to the dad and said something to the effect that his problem was that he (the son) had to always be pushing him (the father) to make decisions to make the farm more modern and more efficient. And he (the son) was getting tired of always having to do that.

<u>When things like this start to happen in a sales encounter, it is best to back out of the sale and let the two people you are selling to discuss the situation between themselves, because if you try to take sides, either way, you will lose.</u>

The father said a few choice words back to his son and the son shot back a few choice words to his father again, only much louder now. The son then asked me how much all this would cost and I told him. That's when I found out instantly they were farming 50/50

What I Learned In Life From A Liquid Manure Pit

because the father piped up and said... "I ain't paying for half of that crap. So you might as well pack up and hit the road mister." The son turned to me and said... "You take that short bolt and long bolt kit across the road to my farm and have my wife write a check for the full amount. And tell her to write you a personal check, not a corporate one. If she has any question, have her call over here." At that point, the father exploded and I was not sure if he was coming at me or his son, but his son was the first person to intercept him.

Then the real fireworks began. The son called him a few names and told him to back off and the father got more furious and started pushing and shouting at him even more. Now I am back peddling as best I can and I had always learned to lay the bolt kit down before you move your truck or you will have a half hour mess to pickup and sort out when it falls off the tailgate. I dropped it flat down in the back of my truck and started to say something apologetic when the son said quite sternly... "Do what I told you and if you have a problem, have her call over here!"

This is when my second most incredible thing happened in my sales career to farmers. After a few more very heated words between them, and some shoving back and forth, the dad took half a swing at the son and the son grabbed him, and within seconds, they wrestled each other to the ground. It was the most unbelievable sight I could have ever imagined. Here was a father and son fighting over my nut and bolt kits. Honestly, I did not know what to do. Then out of nowhere comes this guy's mother, from the house with a broom. She starts hitting the two of them as hard as possible with it and looks at me in between the smacks as if she were thinking.... "What kind of Devil has driven into our yard and caused this horrible thing to happen between my husband and son?"

Soon they stopped, especially after she had gotten in a couple of good licks to both of their heads with the hardbound part of the broom. I think I was in shock when they both got up and started brushing themselves off. That's when the son said to his father... "That does it, we are splitting up this operation today! I am sick and tired of fighting you over everything (I was wondering if they fought like that over a lot of things). His mother started to chime in and his father shut her up instantly by looking at her and saying....

What I Learned In Life From A Liquid Manure Pit

"Good riddance! Good riddance! I don't need him and he doesn't need me."

Well, once more the son pointed to his house but he did not have to tell me what to do this time, I was out of there instantly. When I got to the son's farm, I simply told his wife that he had OK'd this purchase and that's when I realized I did not even have a signed sales receipt to show her. She looked at me strangely, especially when I said everything was going in his shed and she was to write me a personal check, *not* a corporate one.

Without hesitating, I told her to call over there if she was concerned. Well she did and I heard some very interesting comments as she apparently was talking to her mother-in-law. Soon she came out with a check and showed me where to put everything. Then she said.... "What in the world happened over there?" I exclaimed as honest and forthright as I could that... "I showed them both this material we just placed in your barn and they got into a fight over buying it or not. To tell you the truth mam, I think this has been brewing for a long time and I just happened to be the spark that caused the fire today." She shook her head in disgust and went back into the house.

I thought about stopping in town to cash the check for fear it would not clear in a day or two once they both came to their senses. However, something told me the sale was going to hold up. However, the partnership probably was not and that saddened me a bit. Neither the company nor I heard from them as a year passed. Since there was no one covering that territory yet, and I could do some cherry picking, once again I was passing through heading from one area to another, so I veered out of the way and eventually zeroed in on the son's farm.

Since I knew the son would be my friend, and he certainly would need refills by now, I decided to stop and see him. Well there was no pickup truck on his side of the road and sure enough, there were two over at the father's farm like a year ago. Well, I wasn't about to set foot in that father's yard again because my name was dirt over there. So I drove up to the son's house and knocked on the door. His wife answered and I asked for him by name since we had him in our records now.

What I Learned In Life From A Liquid Manure Pit

"I think he is over at his father's place....yep, I see his pickup truck over there." Oh great I thought, here we go again. In parting, I asked her.... "Did they actually break up after I was here the last time?" Suddenly she realized who I was and said... "Oh yeah, that was you wasn't it? Yes, they did break up that day and on the books, they are still farming separate, but only on the books side of it. They made up shortly after they split up and so they still help each other."

"OK" I said, trying to show some remorse, "is it alright if I check his nut and bolt kit and his drill bit set in the shed, to see what he needs for refills?" Sure, go ahead, but you will have to go over there to be paid because he has the checkbook with him. Oh great I thought, there was no way to finesse my way out of it. I was going to have to face the father once again. I checked on the refills needed and he needed quite a bit of them. Then I found his drill bit set and replaced the drill bits broken or missing, and headed across the road.

Sometimes in sales and in life, you have to do what you have got to do, in order to get the job done. Remember, if it were easy, anyone could do it and it takes real courage to be at the top of whatever profession you choose to be in.

As I drove into the yard, at first I did not register with either of them. Then, as I turned sideways to them, they saw the Ace Nut and Bolt sign on the side of my pickup truck doors. They both started walking towards me. I got out and used the son's name and held out my hand. He shook it and said... "I didn't think we would ever see you again. How the heck are yah?" I couldn't believe it, I felt like the prodigal son, at least to the son. Now I glanced at the father who was within a few feet of me now. He spoke and I nearly dropped dead after I heard what he said... "I want one of them nut and bolt sets and a drill bit set too."

After I picked myself up off the ground, I replied..."Great, where do you want them?" I asked. He and his son led me into the pole barn and showed me where to place them. I was so curious as to what was going on, they could probably read my mind. The son spoke up.... "We broke up after we saw you that day but after a couple of weeks we both came to our senses and while we don't have a corporate farm together, we continued to help each other like before. And since I had the nut and bolt kits, whenever we needed a bolt and nut of a particular size, I kept track in round numbers as to what dad would owe me for them, especially if he would have had to run to town (which was easily ten miles distant and those 'in town prices' were very high compared to most of our refills)."

He continued… "The way I figure, he has just about paid for my set of bolts now so I will need you to refill them." I told him I had already taken inventory and I had fixed up his drill bit set so I showed him what he owed me if I placed the refills in his kit. "Excellent, yep, dad sure took care of paying for those refills and then some." The father laughed with his son, which surprised me greatly. I wondered if he had somehow found a heart in the past year.

He headed to the house for a check while the son wrote me one for his refills. "You know"… I said…. "I am glad things turned out like they did. You cannot imagine how many times I have thought about the two of you and the fact that I had caused the two of you to get into a fight over our nut and bolt kits." He laughed again and said…. "No problem, my old man and I have done far better by farming like this. We appreciate each other even more now and you actually did us a big favor that day. That blow up had been brewing for years." I was right then; my incident with them had just been the straw that broke the camel's back that day about a year ago. What a fascinating turn of events.

As I headed down the road that afternoon, I had a big smile on my face. Not because of the money I had just made. It was because I would never have thought all these plusses would have turned out from my visit over a year previous. To this day, the memory of mom hitting those two with a broom has vividly stuck in my mind. I replay it consciously and subconsciously now and then, and since it is one of my favorite stories, I love sharing it with others because once the ole nut and bolt guy visited that particular farm, eventually, after some initial trauma, everything turned out to have a "happy ever after" ending. Life is good.

Chapter 5

Former-Farmers Selling To Farmers, Were Their Own Worst Enemy

I inherited a distributorship and sales force that was mainly former-farmers, or people who grew up around farming. This was a double-edged sword because, not only was this a tremendous advantage for a salesperson, it proved to be a tremendous disadvantage too. The advantage was that no one needed to teach these people about farming, especially in their area. They were knowledgeable and knew their way around. The disadvantage was they thought like farmers instead of salesmen. It took me awhile to discover this fatal flaw we call in sales of being *sympathetic* instead of *empathetic* with your customers.

<u>When you are sympathetic in sales encounters, you get inside the customer's shoes and whatever their current woes, problems or pains are for the day, you absorb them and thereby reduce your effectiveness to sell to them, dramatically. Conversely, when you</u>

are empathetic, you understand where they are coming from, but you don't go there with them!

My first hint that something was amiss was sales records compiled from across the country by telephone and by what came into the home office in the paper trail of orders. It seemed that with the former farmers (which was most of the sales force), their sales were up at about the same time and down at about the same time too, with little variances. My first thought was that it was weather related. However, obviously we were not having the same weather across the many states we served. The distributors and salespeople were not that helpful in solving this until I rode with a salesperson in Wisconsin and we left very early in the morning (dairy farmers can be called on early and late I learned because they milk twice a day).

Shortly after picking me up at my motel, he had the radio on in the background and the market reports came on. All the current (or daily) and future prices (commonly called futures) on everything from livestock to bushels of corn and beans were reported. I really did not understand all that until this salesperson commented.... "Oh great, that is the third day in a row the market has gone down the limit on corn and beans. And livestock is still off too. We will be lucky if we sell one bolt kit today. I was afraid of that with you coming up here to work with me today."

I looked at him and then the radio, and then back at him. "You mean to tell me those kinds of farm reports actually affect these farmers buying decisions?"... I asked, still not tying everything together yet. "You bet it does!".....he responded with great emphasis and a touch of sarcasm in his voice because he felt I should already know this kind of stuff if I am the national sales manager.

Well it didn't take long to see how this negative farm report news affected our sales. My salesperson was *sympathetic* right from the start. He commensurated with the farmer and soon both of them were "singing the blues". It was almost an afterthought that my guy tried to sell the farmer anything and even then, it came across like he was saying... "As bad as things have been lately, you probably don't want to buy anything today, do yah?" Nope, he didn't and just about everyone else that morning did not either. For a while it made me a believer of all this.

I am convinced this problem of not knowing or being trained to recognize the critical difference of being empathetic as versus sympathetic in a sales encounter, has killed countless millions of sales (and continues to do so), that might otherwise have taken place. You have to assume someone eventually got that sale but the untrained salesperson was not the one to do so.

However, it did not take me long to get a note out to everyone about this factor as a warning that mentally, they were whipped coming out of the chute. To my total amazement, it changed virtually nothing. I still could see the trends and now I knew the main, contributing factor. Yes, there were localized factors like droughts or too much rain in an area, but our guys were smart enough for the most part to go work somewhere else when that happened.

It was these negative market reports that were universal and my former-farmers were locked into them each morning like drug addicts. So what about when the markets were up? As you would suspect, sales went up across the country at the same time. It averaged total sales out somewhat but I needed to increase sales, not keep averaging them. What I was baffled about was how do I eliminate this as a problem and make it an opportunity. The solution did not come to me until I began hiring in larger communities around the country that had rural farming nearby.

Sometimes solutions to problems are right under your nose if you will just keep sniffing them out and be ready to act upon them when they come to you like a lightning bolt. Then, do not hesitate making a decision to take action.

The established process for finding and hiring new salespeople for distributors or for the company was quite simple and effective. The company found the most influential newspaper with the greatest circulation within the area and we ran lucrative sounding ads as to the potential income one could earn. And the income figures we advertised were not really inflated if they wanted to work. Remember, a distributor made 40% off of the list price and his salespeople made 30%.

In fact, some of my biggest problems with keeping new salespeople, especially the younger they were, was they made so much money, so fast, they did not know how to manage it and it went to their head. Some would go on a binge of sorts, sometimes never to be found again, and with our materials and money. Our game plan in each territory we wanted to open up was to do interviews at a motel room after running the want ad. Then we would decide on who we wanted to give a try that looked promising and had a decent pickup truck (a requirement in the ad some applicants conveniently overlooked).

Our next step was to line up training days and take these people out with us on cold calls and let them watch. We also had the A/V program so after hearing that ten or more times, they pretty much knew it by heart and did not need it anymore. It only took a short time to tell if we had a promising salesperson or not. If we did, we stocked them with the basics and let them go for a day. They would report back to us at the motel each night as to how they did. Some were so excited about the money they had made that day it was hard to contain them.

I remember one kid in his early twenties coming back to the motel twice for more supplies while I was still interviewing. That one day he cleared in gross income almost $250. He said to me at the end of the day as I gave him his cash for his efforts…. "Wow, my old man barely makes that much in an entire week!!!" Remember friends, this was figures of the early 1970's.

That is when the solution hit me. Even I had gotten into the bad habit of listening to farm reports now and then and while I did not talk about it, they had been down for some time. However, I was dealing with younger people raised in the city, who were not locked into farming as a livelihood. In other words, they did not know any better. They were young and enthusiastic and they sold, and sold and sold while the market kept dropping daily!

<u>As I stated earlier in this book, I learned a long time ago that sincere enthusiasm will sell more products and services than any other sales trait. I had new salespeople setting sales records that had very little knowledge about farming other than what we gave them on a crib sheet to study and to keep them out of trouble. I also</u>

What I Learned In Life From A Liquid Manure Pit

learned in the interviewing process that if they were not enthusiastic, I would pass on them within minutes.

Keep in mind that while the farm reports were a definite indicator as to the root cause of the problem, there were many other negative things that being a former-farmer brought into play. I found that if it was a great day for farming and the farmers were real busy planting, getting hay cut, bringing wheat in or combining the Fall harvest, our former-farmers shied away from contact because they knew they personally would not have wanted to be bothered at that time by a salesperson, if they had been farming. However, if it was raining and no one could work, then the former-farmer salespeople were out there pushing hard. The problem was that many times those were days when everyone went to town for coffee so finding someone home was difficult. I taught non-farming salespeople how to actually capitalize on all of the above.

Over time and even after I moved on to become my own distributor and have my own salespeople and territories, the company and I moved away from hiring former-farmers and gravitated towards people who knew little or nothing about farming. After all, it made sense because I had become extremely successful selling to farmers and I knew enough about farming to hold in my right hand when I started. Personally, when I became a distributor, I never hired a former-farmer and the process worked perfectly. Not to say I did not have my difficulties of hiring and keeping good people all the time. However, this solution to my dilemma was a permanent one and those that followed it in the company, flourished.

There is such a thing in sales as being too smart about everything that is going on to the point that you get into a situation called "Paralysis of the Analysis". You actually process all the reasons why something will not work to the point that it doesn't have a prayer in succeeding. This could not have been truer with my former-farmers.

Chapter 6.

Persistence In Sales Pays Off In The Long Run If You Live To Tell About It

I have a book that gives you the origin of many old sayings passed down through the ages and occasionally it gives you the author too. "If at first you don't succeed, try, try again." ….. isn't one of much fame but it certainly has been around for a long time and it does have some merit, especially when it comes to anything worthy that you are trying to accomplish. In this case, it ended up being worthy. However, it almost cost me life and limb in the process, or so I thought at the time.

Remember how I shared with you earlier that farmers then and now have to farm wherever they can buy or lease land and rarely is all the land connected. Well, I was having a fairly good morning working a township systematically with my plat book, from section to section (a section is 640 acres, which is one square mile, and there are usually at least 36 or more sections in a township). Sometimes the counties were larger and sometimes they were smaller.

All of us salespeople used a valuable sales tool called a plat book to map our way around as we called on farms. We tried to get the latest, most updated copy because the owner's names were on those sections and portions of sections. Therefore, if you saw John Smith owned 400 acres here and 200 there, you could expect he was a serious farmer and a great prospect (however, he could be retired and leasing the land).

I was working in West Central Indiana at the time, very near the Illinois state line, and things had been going well for the last few weeks, and especially for the last few days. Then it happened, I pulled into a guy's farm who I immediately found out hated salespeople with a passion.

I hardly got out of the truck when he came running towards me in a steady trot, and this was a hefty fellow and he had a wrench in his hand. He was pointing and shouting in no uncertain terms to get my butt out of his place and never come back. Well hey, there are always a lot of people who want to hear your message and want to buy what you are selling and I wasn't about to take him on because I might have gotten physically hurt in the process. After all, discretion many times is the better part of valor.

In sales, it is always wise to yield your ground and retreat when your potential customer outweighs you by 50 pounds or more, and especially if he has a wrench in his hand and he is running towards you!

I had a fleeting thought about asking him why he was so upset or maybe finding out if our company had done something bad to him in the past, but that vanished quickly when he stood right outside my open window and pointed to the road. You have to have courage in sales but this kind of encounter will unnerve the best of us and it sure had that effect on me. As I drove down his drive towards the road, my mind was racing about all the possibilities that would make a person so mean and upset like he was. I looked at the plat book again and made a big circle on his name to let me know to avoid his land if I ever ran across his name again because if anyone

What I Learned In Life From A Liquid Manure Pit

was working it, chances were 10 to 1 it would be him. And I did not want to experience that encounter again if I did not have to.

A couple of hours later and two good sales under my belt, I saw a guy coming to an end row or where the fence and the field of crops meet the road. It is a perfect place to get a farmer to stop for a cool one and take a look at your wares. I actually pulled right up to where he would have to make his swing, opened up the back of my truck, and got prepared to invite him over. Yes, you guessed it, I had run across the same guy!

He stopped his tractor and flew off it before I realized it was him. No wrench in his hand this time but he was no nicer than the first time around. However, this time I blurted out something like.... "Hey, I am just trying to make an honest living and I did not know it was you again." At which point he said... "I farm all over this township (he was boasting way too much there I found out later), so if you have a plat book, make damn sure you are reading it before you stop again!"

<u>**Good sales tools are made to be used and be your ally and friend. When you don't use them properly, things will either not happen as they should, or go wrong when you least expect them to do.**</u>

Doggone it, I had not glanced at my trusty plat book before stopping. I just saw a live one and instinctively got prepared for the kill or the sales presentation. Sure enough, as I got back into the cab of my truck, I glanced at the plat book and there was his name, plain as day. Now I was really unnerved. I almost pulled up stakes and drove to another township, and I probably would have, if I had not forced myself to make the next call on a guy that was in his yard as I passed by. Instinctively now, I looked at the plat book out of fear more than for any other reason, even though I could still see the dust of my new found archenemy working his field a half a mile back.

I hit it off instantly with this farmer prospect. He already had somebody else's bolt kit, which we would run into now and then but rarely. However, he let me fill it up anyway, and then we got to talking about this guy as I very carefully asked if he knew anything about him. He smiled a big grin and said... "So you have run across ole Tom Burton (not his real name) have yah? He is a real case as I am sure you must have found out."

He and I talked further and I found out this guy was a loner, not married, and he went through help so fast he had to hire people from two or three counties away. "But what makes him so mean?"... I pressed and my new customer responded... "He lost his wife and daughter in a car accident and to the best of my knowledge, rumor has it they were broadsided at an intersection by a traveling salesman who was drunker than a skunk that day. He has never gotten over that."

<u>As Paul Harvey always says... "And now, the rest of the story." Sometimes finding these things out in sales can help you immensely and sometimes they cannot. However, the more we deal with people, the more we learn not everyone is an open book and not everyone opens up to us right away.</u>

So there it was, the reason for the hatred and apparently, this man continued to take it out on not only salespeople, but also everyone. He was bitter and in a way, due to the fact I knew "the rest of the story" now, I felt sorry for him. However, I also found out this had happened ten years previous and he hadn't let go or healed one iota. I said my goodbye to our new customer and proceeded to head West towards the Illinois state line. I stopped to grab a bite to eat and probably lingered longer than I usually would because I could not get this guy off my mind. Then I decided to make a call home and soon I had killed over two hours.

Mileage wise I was now about ten miles as the crow flies from where I had first encountered this guy and I figured I had left him far behind. And good riddance too. I was no psychologist but it sounded to me like he needed one. But just to be safe, I would check the plat book until I got out of this county and crossed into Illinois and a new county and township.

The last stop I made in Indiana was on a guy who was in a staging area (no house and maybe a small shed with a small yard) and the plat book stated a name I had not seen before. As I got closer, something seemed familiar from earlier that day, but I wasn't sure yet what it was. As I drove into the location where the pickup truck and a tractor were sitting, I could see the toolbox was open on the pickup bed and all I could see under the tractor, due to the bright sun and dark shade, was the legs and part of the waist of this particular farmer.

The pickup truck looked somewhat familiar but it did not register with me as to where I had seen it before. As I always do, I announced myself with a friendly greeting and waited for a reply. To my absolute, total shock, out pops my archenemy one more time! However, this time he isn't shouting or threatening me. He is talking slow and his words came out exactly like this as he stood up... "You know, you have either got to be the most stupid salesperson I have ever met, or the most persistent with a lot of guts. I hate salespeople but if I take a look at what you've got, will you leave me alone once and for all?"

I could not believe it. This guy who had threatened bodily harm to me (or so it seemed) twice before, was now negotiating with me to leave him alone if he finally looked at what I had. Now I remembered the pickup from earlier that day. I gathered my composure quickly, and I mentioned to him his name was not in the plat book for this land. He did not react one iota. Then I quickly went to the back of my pickup, dropped the tailgate and proceed to tell him about what we had. In the process, I had forgotten to offer him anything to drink and when he spotted my cooler, he asked if I had something cold to drink in it. Soon the two of us were drinking a couple of Cokes (no beer for this guy until I was long gone out of his sight).

Once you win an antagonistic customer over, take it real slow and cautious because you are still skating on thin ice with them and you could blow it all in an instant.

Now I have got to tell you, he never was real friendly throughout the sales encounter. In fact, he was probably one of the strangest, most prickly customers I ever sold to for the company. Nevertheless, he bought both of the bolt kits and the drill bit sets. His reasoning was that he was going to put them in his pick up truck because he travels around so much. This was a very smart move for mobile farmers like him so I picked up on the idea and started using it within my sales pitch, whenever it applied.

He admitted, all he had currently was an assorted collection of odds and ends on board with him. When we consummated the deal,

I offered my hand and he nearly crushed it as he turned and walked away (my hand hurt for days). I never saw him again or heard if he ever reordered. Soon that was no longer my territory and at the time, I was kind of cherry picking and establishing repeat customers for the company while making some excellent money. I hope he found some peace down the road because every time I think of him, I realize how much hurt and bitterness a person can carry with them when they will not let go of something. In addition, while he scared me half to death and probably many more like me, he wasn't all that bad in the end. And he got what he wanted and I made some good income in the exchange.

__Persistence in sales does pay off, even when it is an accident like the above story. In my opinion and the opinion of other great salespeople, the really good sales people get going when everyone else has called it quits.__

Chapter 7.

Dress For Success Or At Least Dress For The Part

You never get a second chance for a first impression, *never*. Therefore, in sales, you need to know some critical things about how to dress for different situations, how to be prepared when you are not sure, and how to look sharp at whatever level you dress. In addition, you need to establish a persona that is different from your competition, and even stands out when possible. Also, I learned a long time ago there is a truism in life that you can easily dress down for the occasion, but it is very difficult to dress up if you come in at a much lower level than your customer.

Selling to farmers was a lot like that. I fully utilized these truisms. I carried it beyond the way I dressed to the way I carried myself and the truck I drove into the farmer's yard. When I first met some of the former-farmer old timers out there, I found them to be firm believers that if you drove into a farmer's yard with a flashy, new or good looking, clean pickup truck, the farmer would be envious of you and also think you were making a lot of money off of farmers. Some salespeople and distributors thought junkers type pickup trucks with a little rust and some fenders flapping in the breeze, was just the ticket. They also thought you should never look more successful or even equal to the farmer. Well, that was once again the ole negative, "stinking thinking" as Zig Ziglar calls it.

__In my opinion, when it is all boiled down to the bottom line, people do want to deal with people who look and act the part of success. In addition, if the person's persona is interesting and unique, that helps one even more__.

Bob firmly believed it was just the opposite of their thinking all along and of course, he was right. People want to deal with successful people and when you dress right and look the part of success, people are drawn more to you, both consciously and subconsciously.

Sure, they might be a little envious, but that's okay. The winners I called on in the farming business were already practicing their own style or mode of being a successful farmer. As a rule, as I look back, most of my highly successful farmers had barnyards that were not messy and their sheds and pole barns were clean for the most part. Things looked organized versus having that helter-skelter look. Occasionally a messy farmer was successful but not often in my experience. In addition, if you think about it, our program was selling the concept of being further organized and more effective.

When I first started out in this business, I always wore a good fitting, well made, expensive, light colored, Stetson, cowboy hat, nice leather boots (and well insulated Sorrel boots in the winter), Levi pants and a good western shirt (long or short sleeve depending on the weather). In the winter, I wore a western type coat with a lambs wool lining and real leather skin on the outside. In real cold weather, I wore leather gloves. I always tried to keep my coat open so people could see all the orders bulging in my breast pocket. Sure, I got looks sometimes when I drove into a yard, or stopped into a coffee shop, but it was my persona and they never forgot me once they met me for a number of reasons. I was known wherever I worked as the "Nut and Bolt guy who wears that cowboy hat" and that recognition made me money often. It was my unique Brand.

What I Learned In Life From A Liquid Manure Pit

My flashy, good-looking truck was a beautiful sight to behold and I kept it that way. It was a blue and white one ton, 454 cubic inch engine, Chevy Silverado model, with dual 25-gallon gas tanks and a nice looking blue and white topper on the back. I had a CB with a large antenna that usually stopped moving about one moment after I stopped. The red, white and blue, magnetic flag signs with the company name were added to the side doors of the truck as the crowning touch. When I drove into a barnyard, and stepped out of my truck, there was no doubt I was making a statement. You just had to sit up and take notice.

Sometimes I got snickers and smiles as I stepped out of my truck; sometimes I got outright insulting but usually harmless comments; but most of the time they sat up and took notice. It didn't take long for them to realize once I engaged with them that I was a successful businessperson offering them the opportunity to jump on the bandwagon and do what the rest of their winner neighbors were doing. Sure, as a professional salesperson, I would adjust my personality traits to theirs somewhat, but my over all image and persona stayed the same across the nation.

There were many times in the summer months when it was extremely hot. It was tempting to not wear the cowboy hat and replace it with a cooler, ball cap (one of the seed corn hats of course). However, I also realized that if I did do this, half or more of my persona would be lost instantly. And what seed corn hat would be safe to wear with so many types out there? Other than my boots switching to Sorrels in the winter and my shirtsleeves to a heavy coat when it was cold enough to force me to do so, I found a persona that worked and I stayed with it. Best of all, I loved playing this persona and I really became the person I was playing much like a character actor in plays and movies.

Remember that *if you aren't unique, you had better be cheap.* Except for a rare sale now and then, where I made a definite decision to deal with someone to gain the sale rather than possibly lose it altogether, I was never cheap and I always sold value over price. Later, as I got really experienced at selling to farmers, I developed a tactic to give a farmer of my choosing a fantastic deal which I could afford to do, because there was a real payoff from doing so. I will explain that in-depth more in a later chapter. People do not remember average or below average people they encounter. However, they do remember unique ones, especially if their encounter is a pleasant one. Plus, the real pay off is they will share their encounter with others.

<u>In sales you need to find the base persona and dress that works for you and then adjust or customize it according to the different situations you encounter.</u>

Chapter 8.

Signs, Signs, Everywhere There Are Signs, And Most Times They Mean Pay Dirt

I mentioned earlier that when a farmer had signs warning you to stay away, I always ignored them. In most cases, they definitely put the signs up to keep salespeople away. However, occasionally there would be humorous signs and that made me get more excited because I knew I was about to engage with a friendly kind of person, whether they bought or not (and invariable they did).

Sometimes the "beware of dogs" sign was prominent and the real scary one I will tell you about later towards the end of my book, was the one that said… "Honk your horn, Do Not Get Out of Your Truck". Usually when you pulled into this kind of place, there were one or two mean dogs, usually German Shepherds because Pit Bulls, Rottweilers and even Dobermans had not been developed enough to show up on farms yet. These dogs would be jumping up on the side of your door, snarling and barking incessantly.

Well, I learned in the business early that if you were afraid of dogs or showed *any fear*, you were in a world of hurt, literally and figuratively. Bob had told me you had to get out of the truck, period, so the dogs knew you were not afraid of them. However, he also told me to be the alpha male and always let them know you were in charge. If you showed just one second of fear, they would eat you for lunch. I was not afraid of dogs originally but this job tested that courage twenty times or more a day.

It takes courage to be in sales if you want to make really good money. In fact, sometimes you need to be a little crazy and you definitely have to be a calculated risk taker. Besides the signs that do mean pay dirt, there are danger signs in sales and in life you really do need to pay attention to if you want to survive.

The signs I really loved to see were any kinds that said something about salesmen. Every time I thought I had seen them all, I would run into another one. The most common one was…. "We shoot every third salesman and the second one just left." Those guys were easy hits. Another popular one was… "Absolutely no salesmen." These guys were not going to be as friendly but they never shot you either. Another popular one was…. "Keep Out, Private Property".

Now think about this…every farm is private property. But what is the worst that could happen to you if you drove into their yard? They might try to scare you (which rarely happened to me), but they were not going to shoot you unless you did something totally stupid. Signs were there for a reason, to screen out the meek and only deal with the people who really had something great to sell. Well Okay, that was my reasoning anyway and it seemed to be true 9 times out of 10 if not much more.

Bottom line, these warning signs made me and anyone else in the company, good money. I remember watching a competitor I had been tailing one day. When a distributor got a competitor in his area, he had the option to have the company come out with a few guys and me and surround this guy through a very clever process of selling out in ripples once he began stopping on farmers. The goal was to frustrate this new nut and bolt competitor because everywhere he turned each day, once he got started selling in an area, an Ace Nut and Bolt guy had already been there, sale or no sale. And since these were always good salespeople, a sale was usually made.

The plan was simple and we would borrow or pull together all the salespeople from that distributor to form what I used to affectionately call, "Barnes Raiders". Sometimes, if it was a small distributor, we would pull from other distributors. One of us would be assigned to tail this guy from his home when he started out for the day, and today it was my turn. We would decide ahead of time to set our CB's on a fairly clear channel no one used in the area. Then, when he made his first stop, I would direct the "raiders" to circle out around him and start selling to farmers in a 360 degree circle.

This "Raiders" tactic required the point man staying far back and occasionally using binoculars along with our CB's and it was incredibly effective. This time, I noticed he slowed up at a good looking farm with the pickup in the yard, and then he drove on. As I went by the farm, I noticed salesperson warning signs were posted. I made note for the distributor, or one of his salespeople, to drop back later and see this farmer. It was obvious our competitor wasn't going to stop there and he had one big flaw we could really take advantage of and that was his fear of going onto a farm with warning signs. We already knew this guy was new to the farmer sales business and that observation told me he was an amateur and lacked courage too.

This tactic was always a guarantee that after a few days of frustration, wherever this new guy turned after his first stop, he would run into our salespeople having been there before him. Then he would realize he could not make a living at this new job and he would be done for sure within days or a week at the most. Now, had he been a pro, the job would have been much more difficult and he would have caught on to what was happening and even left his home in the middle of the night to avoid us.

Signs do not have to be physical to scare salespeople away. They can take on many forms from observing a potential customer and fearing his or her personality, to "curb judging" a place of business or farm or home. This is when you would find yourself thinking it was too overwhelming to approach this farm, thereby mentally whipping up on yourself as you become more and more aware of all these negative signs that you are convinced will kill the deal. I was once taught that FEAR breaks down as False Evidence Appearing Real. If you want to be a great salesperson, you need to know this and overcome this false evidence because if you do not, you will never make it big in sales.

<u>Learn how to make signs of any kind your friend in sales</u><u>. **And learn how to read them well**. **Because when you do, you will add to your bottom line significantly**</u>***.***

Chapter 9

Learning To Love The Smells You Once Hated

Anyone who has driven by a large hog, cattle or poultry farm, knows that the smell can be awful, especially when it gets hot and humid with very little air movement. Sometimes, if you drive by a huge operation, once the smell gets in your vehicle, it can stay with you for miles and even linger awhile on your clothes (like when you hit a skunk). Dairy farms can give off an interesting fragrance although they are nothing like the above smells. These wonderful smells have started a lot of problems around the country as suburbs expand into farm areas and people build within sight and smell of these farms that existed long before the developers and homeowners arrived.

Well, like everyone else, before I got into the farm sales business, these smells were really pungent to me. In fact, I must admit there were a couple of times in my first few months where I was within a hair's breath of puking but managed to hold it in until I was done with the farmer. I did learn from Bob that one of the dos and don'ts was to be careful how you treated your travels from one livestock farm to another. The reason was very simple….you could be the spreader of disease from an unhealthy flock or herd to one that was just fine, before you arrived.

It happened often and once that disease started to spread, if it was not nipped in the bud instantly, a farmer could lose a lot of animals and be quarantined while experiencing a lot of expense. Moreover, an entire operation could be wiped out suffering a great financial loss for the farmer, or even bankruptcy. For those reasons, as I became more and more experienced, I was always careful where I walked and what I was doing when it came to livestock. I would even ask permission from the farmer or rancher if I was not sure. They always appreciated that concern shown by me.

Well somewhere along the line, I began to learn to actually love those smells, and the worse the better! You see, unless the market was a total bummer, these farmers usually had ready cash and the neat thing about dairy farmers was they usually got a milk check on the first and fifteenth of the month so the eagle was always flying on those farms. In my opinion, a poultry operation was the worse smell of all. I never walked into the buildings holding livestock unless I was with the farmer and I had protective wear on my feet. Usually, if it was a well run and large operation, the farmer was proud to show me around. That smell, permeated with ammonia, could stay with you for days if you did not do something with it. Whatever town I stayed in, if the motel did not have some kind of coin Laundromat service for the guests, I would locate the nearest one when I was in livestock country. If I did not wash something, at least I would just throw things into the dryer for a few moments, just to air things out.

__If you want to reap the benefits of special sales opportunities, sometimes you will need to sacrifice in ways you never imagined before. And as the ole saying goes… "When in Rome, do as the Romans Do". This kind of behavior builds relationships that last.__

One time I stopped at a very large hog farm operation I could smell miles away because I was downwind of it. Even though I was

What I Learned In Life From A Liquid Manure Pit

a seasoned veteran by now, this place reeked so bad I wondered if the owner was producing some kind of mating fragrance for hogs or something. It was in the 90's and the air was so thick with humidity that smell was reaching a tolerance index of 100 for me. But that smell also meant pay-dirt.

It was all I could do to concentrate on my sales pitch and keep things moving. Wouldn't you know it, this guy was the friendly type (not a cob-roller, he was just friendly) and I could tell he liked me. I had also uncovered a need for what we had to offer him so short of throwing up on him or in the cab of my truck while driving out of his yard, I hung in there for about an hour. Bless his heart, he bought just about everything and I was never so glad to write up that order and finally get going.

Since it was approaching noon and I had eaten quite early that day, I figured once I got out of there, I would break the rule of not working during lunchtime and stop in town (which was only two miles away) and get in an air-conditioned place while airing my lungs and clothes out in the process. I made one big mistake at that point....I mentioned I was headed to lunch now and thanked him for his business. "Hey, don't go eat lunch in town, my wife has lunch ready right about now and we always have room for one more if you don't mind eating with me and a couple of my hired hands?" Oh Lord, how do I get out of this one I thought as he actually put one arm on my shoulder to guide me to the back door of the house. About that time, I saw a pickup truck driving into the yard and the two guys who got out were his fulltime farm hands and he introduced them to me.

Now one thing you do not do in this business is turn somebody down when they offer you a meal or even a gift because it is usually considered a major insult. In addition, if they just bought something from you, it would amplify that insult greatly (I even got some invites to stay overnight when out West where it was mostly ranchers). Remember, I had just said I was headed to town for lunch, dang it. I tried one limp excuse of not wanting to put anybody out and that had no effect on the invitation being dropped whatsoever.

Okay, so I am walking into this house and right into the kitchen, which was not air-conditioned, just a big ole floor fan blowing on us. There was a basin to wash up near the back door and everyone took turns as the farmer introduced me to his wife once I washed my hands and threw some water on my face like everyone else did. She was surprisingly nice looking and did not have the typical farmer's tan or even sunburn. She was definitely a "house lady" and this usually meant a great cook too.

Now here was the dilemma I was facing. Up to this time in my farm sales career, I had never eaten food in this type of overwhelming, pungent aroma. In addition, when you are around that aroma all the time, you just don't notice it anymore. It reminded me of some friends of ours who lived under the approach of the main runway of our local airport, who never seemed to hear the airplanes landing anymore when you visited them. You on the other hand, thought every time a plane landed you were experiencing war games with strafing and a bombing raid starting on their home at any second.

So remember, my stomach is reaching that 100-tolerance index of throwing up and the main course is served to me immediately before anyone else! It was some kind of pork fixing looking a lot like a stew with sweet corn and green beans mixed in it. She had also set out some mashed potatoes and gravy on the side, and cornbread, butter and ice water! Any other time I have to tell you, this would have been my kind of meal. But under the circumstances, I wasn't feeling too good. I broke out into a cold sweat, and hoped they did not notice. I said a silent prayer for myself while my new customer gave grace for all of us.

I was about to panic now because everyone was digging in and I was sitting there with a full serving of everything directly in front of me, buttering my cornbread to stall a little longer. I prayed again and drank some water. I mean to tell you, I have always had an inherited stomach reflex problem when it came to digesting food and so I was not sure if my breakfast was getting ready to come up or what. The sweat intensified on my forehead but everyone was digging in and talking as they ate. My new customer was telling his guys what he had just bought. But that's when I noticed the Mrs. was watching me now because I had not dug in yet. Just as I was about to try the first bite making sure I had a clear shot to the back door if I was about to

What I Learned In Life From A Liquid Manure Pit

lose my breakfast, my new farmer friend asked me to tell everyone, one of my humorous stories I had told him earlier out in the yard.

I jumped on the chance to stall eating and a strange thing happened. As I got deeper and deeper into one of my favorite stories (a chapter yet to come), and the sincere laughter started, my mind got totally off my upset stomach and the overwhelming stinch. One story led to another request and I became the entertainment for lunch. Talking so much was a perfect excuse for not eating as fast as they were. Now I was actually taking a few bites and doggone if it wasn't very good. They were now having seconds. Story telling definitely helped me make the sale earlier, combined with many other important things in sales. However, for sure it saved me a great embarrassment at their lunch table.

Finally, we wrapped up and everyone was having a good time. I am sure this day they took more time at their meal than normal. You see, when you are a traveling salesperson and a good storyteller too, people love hearing the stories. And they loved to know what I heard was going on around the country. You were like a traveling, live, farmer's newspaper. I left that farm feeling great and to tell you the truth, I noticed the smell again while in the yard but not enough to bother me then or ever again.

Pay dirt in sales can come to you in many ways like learning to live with the unpleasant conditions that mean money in your pocket if you endure. It also helps to be a great storyteller; sometimes they should relate to the sales situation and sometimes they can just entertain, especially if you already have the order.

Chapter 10

What I Learned In Life From A Liquid Manure Pit

This is my favorite story of all of my four and a half years in the farm sales business. In addition, this event made me more money by "word of mouth" than any other time in my life in sales. Combined, it is the most funny and the most embarrassing story I tell. That is why my wife Judy felt this story should be the title of my book, and as a marketing expert, she felt it was catchy too and she was right. Well, it happened this way one very cold winter day in an area in northwestern Indiana.

I was working by myself out of a fairly inexpensive (okay, cheap) motel. I felt I was becoming a veteran now and this was my first winter in the business. Bob had taught me earlier that if you talk to the owners of the hotel and tell them you do not want your room cleaned and only fresh towels when you asked for them, you can negotiate a much better daily or weekly deal than paying the normal daily or weekly rate. Even though I usually headed home Thursday night or early Friday morning because I would hit my sales goal and be ready to do so, these savings added up. And after all, I did not get sheets and towels changed at home more than once a week anyway.

It had been very cold for three days running hovering around a high of 10 to 15 degrees and it was towards the end of January. There wasn't much snow on the ground for insulation, so ponds and rivers were really frozen solid and thick. I was getting my first real indoctrination of working in bitter cold weather so I dressed accordingly in layers including long underwear. Now you have to remember, Bob could not teach me everything about farming in just one day of driving to Sioux City, Iowa. As you have found out in this book so far, some things I had to learn by trial and error from then on (with the emphasis on error).

In addition, since I was about seven months into this business, while my learning of totally new things got less and less in frequency, either because I did not notice it before or for whatever the reason, I would occasionally run across a new thing and absorb it for future reference. Each time that would happen, I would always be very careful to finesse myself in the conversation so as to appear to have already known the new thing being discussed and learned by me. Boy would I have loved Google and the Internet back then. I would have been researching things about farming every night in my motel room.

It is important to learn everything you can about the industry you are selling to so that you are well prepared and do not get yourself in trouble or look stupid. Back then, I might have had some excuses but today, there would be none with all the research tools we have at our disposal.

Well, the title of this book and this chapter is a good hint of where this tale is headed. For some reason, up until that first seven months or so, I had never really taken notice of a liquid manure pit, nor examined one up close (which I soon would be able to state I was an expert on them within a few moments). I realize subconsciously I saw them previously but up until now, there was no reason for me to ever get near them to investigate them close up.

What I Learned In Life From A Liquid Manure Pit

To explain further to those of you who have never been around one, basically it is a large concrete pit that is usually four feet to six feet deep with a dirt ramp going up the one or more sides of it. This is where the manure is carried by a piece of equipment that has had this wonderful stuff pumped into a tank or even in a more crude method, a front loader. Later, when it is more convenient, this manure is pumped or loaded into a manure spreader and then spread on the fields for fertilizer. As far as I know, both then and certainly now, there were some restrictions on putting this liquid manure on fields where sweet corn or direct human consumption crops were being grown. Whether or not farmers followed that rule of thumb and guidance back then was another matter.

So the stage is now set. I know nothing about these liquid manure pits and it has been very cold in the area I had been working in, for three days now. Oh, one more thing….liquid manure will eventually freeze, but it has to be subjected to a lot of very cold subfreezing weather or even sub zero weather for days to set up at all. However, one thing I did not know was that it has a built in heat generator by its chemistry make up. As this manure decomposes, it generates gases and heat. So, while at first glance, you may think you are looking at a solid surface, then again it may not be! Don't get ahead of me now.

While it had been an average week so far sales wise, this was Wednesday now and I had not made a sale yet that morning. I reasoned it to be the prolonged influence of a combination of the weather, the market being off slightly and people just not wanting to talk to me out in the cold. Occasionally a farmer would have me back into their heated section of the pole barn if there was room so we could get out of the bitter cold.

Everyone who saw me, remarked that only the real salespeople worked on days like this and of course, that worked in my favor and I would play that up to the hilt when I could. (As a distributor, I taught my guys to work on miserably bad days because no one else did and I also had them work Christmas Eve because wives were always looking for something else to buy their husband). Well, anyway, I was using the plat book and came upon what appeared to be a huge farm that was more like a ranch. It had signs of supporting lots of

What I Learned In Life From A Liquid Manure Pit

beef cattle and I found the main operation immediately. While there were a couple of pickups in the yard, when I knocked on the door to the pole barn and went into a nicely warmed section draped off with some kind of tarp and heated with what are called salamander or portable heaters, there was no one in there.

Next, I walked back outside and that's when I thought I heard some human voices in the direction of this big concrete, above ground, swimming pool type structure I would later learn to call affectionately, a liquid manure pit. The problem was, the walls were tall enough that I could not see over them. As I mentioned in my description earlier, there was a ramp going up the side of it and it appeared many traces of manure had been tracked by some piece of equipment, going up and down that ramp. I immediately figured out they must dump manure in there. Unfortunately, I did not think this thing through further as I climbed the ramp. Remember, I said, don't get ahead of me.

It didn't take long for me to rise high enough on that ramp to see over the pit wall and notice two guys talking to each other on the other side of the pit, which was maybe 75 feet wide at the most. I shouted at them and they acknowledged back with a wave. Now I have got to tell you, just like earlier in this book when I had that run in with that Charolais bull, I was about to embark on the shortest distance between two points to make a sale, or at least begin the process of doing so! Why would I do something as stupid as that you ask? Because of these factors: (1) very cold weather for days had frozen everything solid in sight (2) ignorance on the part of the salesperson about the chemistry of liquid manure, even if it looks solid, and (3) the realization that to get these guys to buy something, I needed them to come to me or me go to them. I chose to go to them because in front of me there was totally solid ground....or so I thought.

The exposed concrete wall at the top of the pit, had allowed the liquid manure to freeze solid. Even though it looked solid to me, I wasn't sure exactly what I was looking at so I did take one good test with my foot and it was rock solid. So, without further ado, I began to walk across the pit without giving it another thought. The farmers were so shocked they did not stop me in time and in my defense, if

What I Learned In Life From A Liquid Manure Pit

there is any, even though ice on a pond, lake or river can look the same at two inches thick or two feet thick, this stuff looked like solid ground to me all the way across to them.

Boy was I wrong about that one big time! It was very solid and held my 230 lbs of weight for my first two strides (or about eight feet from the edge). However, just as I heard them shout at me to stop, I hit the thinner manure and I broke through sinking to by armpits instantly. I heard a few cuss words as those two headed around the pit to get to me. I was dumfounded and still had not taken in exactly what had happened to me. Reflecting back later that day, I realized that if I had been really unlucky and they had not been around that day, I might have gone just a little too far out and gone totally under. What a horrible death that would have been!

Well once again in my life, God was watching over me because these guys had been there and they got to me quickly with the end of a long rake or pole. They told me to grab on and pull myself out (these guys were smart enough not to even get out on the well frozen stuff when they came to my rescue). I carefully used the pole to turn around and face them (not an easy task I might add). Now that the danger was over, they were starting to laugh as I came out of this mess. Slowly but surely I slid out of this awful liquid manure and you cannot imagine the sight they saw and the mess I had created for myself! For some reason, this stuff was all colors but there seemed to be a predominant yellow and brown color running throughout the stuff coated to every part of my clothing, and it was coating me about an inch thick with bigger globs here and there. Honest, the smell was not that bad at first because it was so cold out. The awful smell would come later.

These two tried to restrain their laughter as we headed to the heated area of their shed. Finally, one of them asked me "What the heck were you thinking?" and he added.... "Man, you could have drowned out there if we had not been around!" Once again, my pride would not allow me to admit I had no idea I had blundered into a mess because I did not know what I was doing. My enthusiasm to sell product drove me to make a move I was now regretting in more ways than one.

What I Learned In Life From A Liquid Manure Pit

I quickly came up with a story that was partly true. I told them I had "been around these pits when they were thawed, but I figured with all the prolonged cold weather we had been having and the look of the pit surface, it was safe to cross". That's when one guy exclaimed to me… "Man, due to chemical reactions in the manure, these things never freeze that solid!" Then he added… "I bet you won't ever do that again. I think everything you have on but your cowboy hat is ruined."…he chuckled, and he had that right for the most part as I quickly found out later, back at the motel.

At that point, once we got into the heated shop, the other guy took an unhooked hose hanging in the air over a rope (keeping the water out so they could hook it up and use it whenever they wanted to in cold weather) and hooked it up to a well head type faucet with a handle that I had seen many times before. He asked me if it was OK to slowly hose me down since I was already wet from all the manure. I readily agreed because there was no way I could sit in the cab of my pickup truck until I got cleaned up a lot. As he did this, the heat in the shop mixed with the instant humidity began to bring another smell I will never forget to this day. It was awful and once again in my farm sales career, my puke index was reaching 100. Only this time, for some reason, I knew it was going to win out eventually. My dignity was shot all to heck but the show must go on.

<u>Sometimes you are hit with what seems like insurmountable setbacks in your sales encounters, but if you will hang in there, they might just turn around quickly and be a real plus for you</u>. <u>Farmers called that… "Making a silk purse out of a pig's ear"</u>.

I thanked these guys after I was fairly hosed down and somewhat dried off and I asked if I could come back when I was cleaned up, "like maybe tomorrow?"….I said. They said "sure" still half-laughing. As I walked to my truck, I surmised that my leather coat was totally ruined. I might be able to save my Levi pants, two shirts, and long underwear, but my gloves seemed hopeless and maybe even my Sorrels were in serious jeopardy. Everything on me but my hat was still wet and well permeated with that horrid liquid manure. I jumped into my truck cab, fired up the engine and headed back to the motel.

What I Learned In Life From A Liquid Manure Pit

I was already nauseated a couple of miles away, as the heater of my truck kicked in and the aroma swirled in the tight quarters of the cab. I quickly opened the windows for some relief. However, that move nearly froze me to death instantly and it really did not help that much. Soon I got very sick. I quickly pulled over and left my breakfast by the side of the road. I think it was so cold, my breakfast froze within seconds of hitting the ground as I tried to gather my composure.

Finally, I got back into my truck, finished driving back to the motel and began a more thorough clean up process. I somehow managed to save my Sorrel boots temporarily, with a lot of work, but while they looked OK, whenever they got hot from then on, that awful smell returned with a vengeance, especially when I took them off at night. Eventually, a few weeks later, I had to give in and buy a new pair. My leather coat and wool lining was history since I always wore it open. My gloves were shot, but I presoaked my shirt, pants, long underwear and socks in the bathtub before heading to the local Laundromat and I was able to save them.

Well once again, as Paul Harvey says, here is the "Rest of the Story" and one of the many reasons why it was such a great learning experience for me in life, and in sales. I chose not to go back to their place the next day after all. In fact, I felt this was enough humiliation for one week, and while it had not yet been a good week cash wise, heavy snow was predicted with more cold weather coming, and my coat was basically useless. So, I packed up later that afternoon and headed home. I recovered quickly and when I arrived home much earlier than normal, I told the story to my wife and a few friends and we all had a good laugh or two. Then the next week I headed back to work in that same area with a new set of clothes and a duplicated new coat I still have to this day.

Since I had missed farmers closer to the motel the previous week, I started hitting them first before working my way back to the place were I had fallen into the liquid manure pit. The weather had moderated slightly with the temperature in the mid twenties and the sun was shining. That's when an amazing thing happened. When I pulled into the very first farm I called on about five miles from the Liquid Manure Pit incident....the farmer recognized the sign on the truck and my cowboy hat (and hey, who knows, maybe my persona). He had heard the story about me already at one of the local coffee shops in town where farmers usually gather! He laughed aloud and I admitted it was me and that I had really pulled a dumb stunt. However, once he got himself under control, he looked at my wares and he bought. Hmmm I thought to myself, that was easy. The story broke the ice with him and built rapport with him instantly.

<u>Amateur salespeople do not take the time to build rapport and set the customer at ease before they start pitching their wares while professionals salespeople realize it is a critical success factor and spend as much time as necessary.</u>

Then I headed to the next farm about a mile North and this guy was looking at me strangely right from the beginning as I got out of my truck. I thought we were not hitting it off at first but what he was thinking about was the exact reason why he did not open up to me at first. Then like an "aha" experience, he asked me with kind of a Cheshire grin… "Are you that crazy salesperson everyone is talking about who nearly drowned in that liquid manure pit last week?" Ouch, now that hurt. Here we had two farmers in a row, not more than a mile apart, who had heard about my blunder. What else could I say but yes? He laughed, I told some more humbling stories like my bull story and he bought. It seemed that Liquid Manure story spread faster in that area than the cry that "The British Were Coming!...and it was definitely getting embellished each time I heard it.

I never corrected people when they told me an embellished version of the story because as long as I kept eating humble pie, they kept buying and having a good time in the process. It was a phenomenon I milked as long as I could in that area. Then it became my favorite tale to tell during a sales encounter, at the appropriate time. For obvious reasons, it worked for me as long as I was in the farm sales business. Today, when I am asked to share stories about this incredible period of my life, I always work this funny story into the conversation somewhere. And both farmers and non farming people alike seem to love it. Of course, the farmers love this story much more because they know all about liquid manure pits and exactly what I had experienced.

You need to be a great story teller in sales and you need to know the appropriate time to use them, and the appropriate tale to tell. Once you have the sale, as I mentioned in a previous chapter, you can entertain your audience, but don't over do it. Leaving them wanting more is the correct approach. Or, as they say in public speaking—"Be bright, be brief and be gone" and leave them laughing too while you are at it.

Chapter 11

The Different Things I Learned About Grain, Livestock And Dairy Farmers

—⚒︎—

Once again, I have to admit my knowledge of different kinds of farmers and farming was somewhat nebulous to me prior to getting into this farm sales business. Sure, I knew a dairy farm when I saw one and I was aware of hogs and beef cattle in my travels as a common city slicker, but that was about as far in depth as it went. As I think back now, when I was a youngster visiting my relatives' farms in central Illinois and southeast Missouri, they did a little bit of everything including having a few cows, hogs and chickens (which was pretty common back then). In the mid 70's and even more so today, you could not be all things to all people when it came to farming so you needed a specialty or niche to focus upon and develop an expertise.

Once I got into the farm sales business, I quickly learned there were many different types of farming and you needed to know how these differences would have an effect on the overall sale. For instance, I found out real quick when I was in dairy country that I could start working very early, even before sun up, and end my day after dusk or the last milking. I also learned these were usually very friendly people as a rule and they were always getting ready cash twice a month for their milk.

Probably my best, most reliable customers came from this group because they used so many nuts and bolts and they were around all kinds of acidic conditions that would destroy the common iron bolt. They loved our dycrominated bolts and nuts that were made of hardened five-grade steel because they did not rust and they did not stretch or break easily like iron ones did.

Of my few invites to stay overnight after eating dinner with them, dairy farmers were the ones who asked me to do it the most. If I was out West and it was getting dark, ranchers always extended the invitation and unless I had to move on, I accepted their offer. Towards the end of the book there is a story that revolves around staying at the homestead of one such rancher. As you have learned from me by now, being invited to lunch and dinner was very common if they liked you and the time was right.

Dairy farmers and livestock farmers would plant and use their own crops for feed as much as possible because they did not want to be subject to the going market prices of the day. The more beautiful "Blue Tube" silos or Harvestors silos you saw on a farm, the better heeled this farmer probably was because those things were very expensive over regular concrete block silos. In addition, the larger their herds, the more of those silos you needed (these special silos could store silage or other feed without allowing it to spoil until you wanted to use it with your livestock). As a rule, the cleaner the operation, the more efficient and the more prosperous the farmer would be, and they bought more products each time you called on them.

One time our company had ordered promotional ballpoint pens by the thousands. Distributors could buy as many or as few as they wanted and I had my share. It had our toll free number on it and since the home office tracked who called on whom, if a farmer reordered in your assigned territory, over the phone, the distributor

What I Learned In Life From A Liquid Manure Pit

got the sales commission for the order (less shipping and handling expenses). Well another learning experience was about to occur. I had only glanced at the clever cartoon Bob had asked be on the pens. It was a bolt chasing a nut and the saying underneath said... "Let's get together and (yep, you guessed it)." .... or something like that. The problem was that it was lewd. Honestly, I never gave another thought about it after I purchased the pens and I had handed out hundreds to this point. That was until the following event unfolded.

I was in northern Indiana in Amish country and I found out quickly that if you won over one Bontrager or Yoder (like Smith or Jones), you were somehow connected up with an entire clan eventually. There were also two types of Amish...those that used modern machinery and those that did not. Then you had the Mennonites who were strictly traditional with no modern conveniences. Either way, whether they were farming 80 acres or 4 to 5 hundred acres, they needed our nuts, bolts and tools.

The traditional Amish and Mennonites farmed like my relatives did in that they had livestock, a few dairy cows and grew corn (and they of course had their horses and buggies). Well I had just made a wonderful sale to a more contemporary or so called modern Amish dairy and grain farmer and I thought without thinking, why not give a pen to each one of his ten kids who had been gathering around us (ranging from about three years old to a few teenagers), while I pitched my wares to him. For some reason, I forgot to give him one of those pens. So, I thanked him for his business, packed up and I drove down his driveway and reached the next farm within just a couple of moments.

Before I could even get past my warm up with my new prospect, here comes a pickup truck barreling up his driveway at full speed. My brand new customer from the last farm jumped out of his pickup and threw the ink pens I had just given his kids, right at me with some words of disgust (not cuss words mind you, but disgust). He said he had half a mind to have me come back and pick up the stuff I just sold him, and refund him his money.

As I picked up one of the pens out of the dirt somewhat in shock, and looked at it closely, the saying and cartoon hit me like a hammer between the eyes for the first time. I had just given a rather lewd handful of pens to a very religious family. I apologized profusely and tried to make up some lame excuse about never really paying attention to what was on the pens but that did not fly at all. Then I did a "disarming tactic" by grabbing an easy out set he had looked at earlier, but had not bought, and I gave it to him free to make up for my blunder in some way. I apologized again, asked for him to forgive me and then asked him what else I could do to make all this right. He took what I gave him and said... "Nothing". Then he got in his truck and drove off, certainly more settled down now than when he arrived.

I turned to my new prospect who I had just met and he was grinning from ear to ear kind of chuckling to himself. He had not said a word as that event played out but he had picked up one of the pens from the dirt and had read the slogan under the cartoon. He said to me... "I think that's funny but I also can tell you why he was so upset. He is an elder of his church. He must have wanted what you sold him real bad or you could have lost the entire sale over these pens."

I agreed profusely and now that the ice had been broken with my new prospect, and an excellent, live referral of what I had to sell, had just witnessed its value in front of him despite my stupidity, I got into my presentation, closed on each item and he bought everything his neighbor had. Oh and you guessed it, he forced me to throw in an easy out set in the process. From that day forward, I was very careful who I gave those pens out to and once I was done with the ones I bought from the company, I did not order any more of them.

Sales aids and advertising novelties can be a wonderful tool to help you get more business and promote more sales. However, you need to consider your audience when you order such things and you need to distribute them with prudence.

Grain farmers are a unique breed. These are farmers who usually do not mess around with livestock and therefore seem to have more time on their hands once the crops were planted. I do not want to imply they were done and no longer busy after planting, and only had to wait for the harvest after that. Besides planting, they needed to do fertilizing, cultivating and weed spraying for soybeans, field corn, wheat, barley, Milo or sorghum, sunflowers, and so forth. I

What I Learned In Life From A Liquid Manure Pit

made it a habit to catch these guys at end rows when they were busy cultivating or cutting or combining. If you had the guts and were bold enough, you could walk right up to them as they reached the end of the field and were ready to turn around or unload the grain they had just harvested, into a truck.

I got to know a younger farmer once and befriended him enough that he actually allowed me to ride a couple of rounds with him. This was a big, twelve row corn combine. I casually implied I would love to try driving it and he agreed to allow me to do so. I catch on to these types of things quickly and knew that since he was working by himself, he had placed his big dump truck strategically in his rounds. So, when you got to a truck, you made the dump into it if the hopper was full (which I was even allowed to do). Later in life, I would learn how to drive a semi truck pulling and parking a 53-foot trailer, but this was far more fun to me for some reason.

I never tried planting and did not want to because I found keeping that guide for a straight line much more difficult than it looked when I rode with a farmer once, on the side of his tractor, while talking to him. Some of this equipment then and now was enormous. One of the problems I learned with huge equipment was the packing down of the soil way too much over a period of time. So there is a trade out as to how big you want to go for the maximum efficiency. Otherwise, you need to do some major tilling of the soil between crops. But the rule of thumb for the most part was.... "bigger is better".

I shocked a farmer once who was picking corn with the exact same green monster (John Deere twelve row combine) by jumping up on his combine and yelling at him to take a break, have a cool one, and look at what I had while I took the next pass at his field. He believed me when I said I could operate it because remember, my persona said to him that I must be some kind of former-farmer or had come from that type of background. He passed on the offer. However, he set the brake and kept it running in neutral, while he stopped and looked at what I had.

He was busy but he was decisive, and he bought right away. I used that tactic more than once and only got one offer to take a pass with a smaller eight-row combine. But it looked the same and I was crazy enough then to do it if the farmer would let me. It was a guaranteed sale of some kind if they got off the tractor or combine so I loved making the offer. I doubt that a former-farmer working for us would have ever done that, even though I know they most likely could have.

I found it to be an incredible, disarming tactic that allowed me to get farmers to stop long enough to take a look at what I had. When combining, since the days are shorter in the fall, they would work at night with lights. I had never run one with the lights on but I reasoned to myself... "How much harder could it be than in daylight?" However, while I would make the offer, quite frankly, I am glad I did not have to find out how different or difficult it would have been.

It never hurts to be very familiar with your customer's line of business because it cuts through the credibility gap instantly. It also lets them know you must really know their business.

Farmers who strictly farmed grain, had little to do after harvest time. So I figured out that these guys were great to call on from then until Spring. However, once Spring came and the fields dried out, they became antsy to get started much like a birddog headed to a hunt. So planting definitely was the most difficult time to get their attention. Of course, the next toughest time to call on them after planting season was when they were harvesting their crops. Remember earlier in my book about the farmer who watched his corn and wheat be destroyed by a hail storm. The wheat was days from being harvested and he missed his chance. The corn on the other hand, while almost totally lost as a grain crop, probably was salvaged some by cutting the remaining stalks and half grown ears of field corn into silage for feed. I never saw that done but I heard it was possible.

I also learned that when you cut hay, you had a time limit then to let it dry in the field, and then bale it and get it into the barn, before it rained again. If in the meantime, the hay got wet by an unexpected rain, that caused problems. When wheat is ready to harvest, you need to get it in as quickly as possible because that is when it is the most susceptible to some kind of weather damage. This grain challenge list goes on and on but quite frankly, if I had been a farmer, I would have chosen grain farming. The main reason is because of

What I Learned In Life From A Liquid Manure Pit

the freedom you had in the off-season other types of farming did not offer like dealing with livestock, especially dairy farmers.

Hogs and Beef cattle presented many variables and challenges of their own. I will never forget the first time I called on a farmer with about four hundred head of beef cattle in fields around his place. He was definitely not in a good mood and since I tried to avoid negatives, I really had not noticed how much the market was down for beef cattle over the last month or so. He pointed to the cattle and said... "Most of these cattle have been ready to go to market for weeks and the price keeps dropping. Everyday I keep them I lose more on them because they are at their prime and will not get any better for the market."

I empathized with him but I did not sympathize with him for fear of him not looking at my wares but he continued to lament about his "horns of dilemma" situation. If he sent them to market now, he would lose a lot of money, and if he held onto them any longer, they will eat him out of house and farm, unless the price recovered dramatically and immediately. His back was against the wall and he had a ton of money tied up in those cattle and was trapped in what seemed to me like a "no win" situation.

I asked very carefully if it would make sense in selling a portion of them and he kept looking at the cattle with no answer. Well, having run into this no win, "catch 22" situation before, I was already there so I asked him if he wouldn't want to take a look at what I had because I was sure he had been through this before and his farm would go on. He turned to me and said point blank... "If this does not turn around soon, me and a lot of other cattle farmers across this nation are going to go under and I won't need anything from you because then there will be an auction."

Wow, now that was a tough objection to handle so I offered him a "cool one" and he accepted. Two hours later, which I could not or should not have afforded him that much time, he bought a set of the smaller drill bits and some hacksaw blades. I cashed the check in town later that day because he had convinced me he was in a world of hurt. The check cleared with no problem so I felt a little guilty.

The cattle market like the grain market, did turn around in a few more weeks, and almost recovered to where it should have been within a month. However, based on what this guy was telling me, I figured it was too little, too late, for the majority of the cattle farmers who had most, if not all of their cattle mature for market a month or two earlier. Sadly enough, three months later, I was cutting across his township to double back to call on a farmer I had missed previously and went out of my way to drive by his place on purpose, just to see how he made out. The farm looked vacated.

I hit the farm five miles down I had missed previously on the plat book and found out the auction had been last week! I felt bad for the guy and it reminded me again that farming is a tough and touchy business and back then, I saw more agony than joy from livestock farmers, because they had absolutely no control over the market. In addition, unlike sitting on grain, everyday they sat on livestock that was mature and ready for market, they were losing money because they had to keep feeding them. And unless the prices rebounded and went way up, they lost that extra feed cost permanently during the wait.

Rarely did livestock farmers hit the market at the correct price but when they did, there was a lot of money to be made. I did find out later in my travels that there were some definite ways to not beat these odds when prices were down, but at least break even or make a little money, while waiting for the next go around. It was a gamble nevertheless, but the smarter the gambler, the better the over all results would be.

In every industry, there is a variety of the types of people you call on and there is a wide variety of their particular needs and wants. Knowing this helps you to be wiser in your approaches towards obtaining the sale. But you need to always be emphasizing with your customers while avoiding sympathizing with them.

Chapter 12

Guts, Persistence And Courage Can Make Things Happen In Your Favor.

I have lost track over the years of the many interesting and downright scary trials and tribulations I went through during this four and a half year saga. I have shared some of the more memorable ones with you already. Later in the book I will get into a few more but in this chapter, I want to focus on the ones that made me money when I hung in there and showed no fear. The following is an incredible adventure that allowed me to share my story in a particular county so often, it just about disarmed and relaxed every farmer I dealt with once I really started knowing how to utilize the story to my best advantage.

Here is what happened one time while I was working in a county in North-Central Indiana. It was a county where the military contracted with farmers to grow hemp plants for use in making rope during WWII. For those of you who do not know, for all practical purposes, while this plant originally came from Asia, back then it was used for making canvas, rope and even paper and cloth. It was also a narcotic drug when smoked, chewed or drunk. Obviously today, we call it marijuana, weed, Mary Jane and lots of other interesting names.

Well, I was working in this particular township one hot day when things were really growing due to the temperature and humidity (there had been plenty of rain). I had no idea this hemp, once planted many years ago, just could not be totally eradicated. It grew wild in ditches and just about anywhere it wanted to. Sometimes people would take the seed and go out into a farmer's cornfield and grow a batch of marijuana, and then harvest it before the combines came. In addition, every teenager for hundreds of miles around had heard about this stuff growing wild and since they knew what it looked like, they would do their best to sneak into this county and do a hit and run harvest when they located some plants. Honestly, back then, I did not know what this stuff looked like and I never inhaled it either. I was oblivious to all this until this day progressed into late morning, approaching noon.

I was running a bad streak of luck of finding anyone home. And with this great, almost perfect growing season with corn now getting way up there in height of eight feet or more, I had trouble seeing if a pickup truck was at the farm I was about to call on, let alone see the next farm, without driving down the road and into their driveway. I had just finished hitting my fifth farm in a row with no one home (I found out later there was a huge farm auction ten miles away which had drawn just about everyone). I was beginning to wonder what was up as I turned south on a nicely graded gravel road and got up to about 50 mph. At the same time, I was carefully looking at my trusty plat book for the next farmer to call on.

That is when I happened to glance up and notice a State Trooper or County Mounty patrol car headed my way at break neck speed, with his lights flashing, and the dust flying. Knowing these roads are fairly safe and wide for two people to pass on them at normal speeds, especially when they are freshly graded, I starting slowing down and moving over to let him pass on by. I planned to slow down to 20 mph or so by the time he blazed past me (I had reached about 60 mph when I first saw him), so I kept moving south towards him. When he was about 100 yards in front of me, he did a crazy thing right out of the movies. He slid to a halt and turned sideways to block the road. But what happened next was the most exciting part yet. He got out of his car, and crouched behind the hood, while pointing a gun in my direction! Now no one had to tell me this was an unusual situation. I slammed on my brakes, they locked up on the loose gravel, and I slid about fifty to seventy five feet closer to him.

Just then, for some reason, my eye caught the image in my left driver's side rear view mirror of more flashing lights bearing down on me from behind! What in the world was going on? Many things raced through my mind in those few seconds as my adrenalin started to surge. To make matters worse, it suddenly dawned on me that for whatever reason these cops were penning me in (it turned out to be County Mounties from that county), I was about to possibly have my truck searched.

No, I was not picking the marijuana plants. Remember, I knew nothing about this ongoing problem until this day. The problem was that I was illegally concealing a loaded, Smith and Weston, 357 magnum, six-inch barrel pistol with hollow point bullets behind and under the rear double cab seat (always within my reach). I carried it for protection due to the large amount of checks and cash I had on me daily (I never left any money or checks in my motel room for obvious reasons and if I had a bank account open in an area, I would deposit most of it just so I did not push my luck).

Now the sheriff deputy behind me jumps out of his vehicle and assumes the same stance with his pistol drawn! Do I get out? Do I stay put? What was I supposed to do? The popular TV series COPS and Bad Boys song wasn't around in those days and I had no personal experience with this kind of thing. And worse yet, there had been nothing like this in the training manual! I stayed put and after a few scary moments, the cop in front of me seemed to be shouting at me and he gestured to me to get out of the truck with my hands up. You have got to be kidding me I thought. Did some one call them and tell them something was stolen from their farm as I was making the rounds (seeing no one but these two guys for the last two to three hours)? I got out of my pickup truck with my hands in the air and they both moved in, with their guns still drawn.

What I Learned In Life From A Liquid Manure Pit

As they both got closer, I could see the tension in their eyes and all three of our adrenaline levels were surely at a maximum now. I began talking fast and asking with a high-pitched voice, which I did not recognize… "What's wrong officers?" One of them shot back in an accusatory way as he holstered his weapon… "You been picking some marijuana today?" I responded in total disbelief…. "Marijuana? Are you kidding me, I am a nut and bolt salesman." As they reminded me to keep my hands in the air, they asked if I would walk to the back of the truck. Then they asked me to open the topper and tailgate and further asked me if it was all right to "search your truck?" "Sure" I said… not trying to show any fear or worry about that loaded gun up front under the back seat. "Can you please tell me what this is all about?"

When the one cop was satisfied there wasn't any fresh cut marijuana in the back of my truck, he climbed out and said… "We got a call that somebody wearing a cowboy hat in a blue and white pick up truck with a topper on it was harvesting marijuana plants from the ditches and you fit that description to a 'T' don't you think?" "Uh yes, I guess so, but they are totally wrong and I have no idea where they came up with that idea."… I said, gathering my courage. Now I was really confused. Had someone done this as a cruel, and maybe even potentially dangerous joke? But what could I say; I did fit the description perfectly. Now came the even more scary part since I knew they were going to ask for the usual identification and registration. We headed to the front of the truck. Both of them had holstered their weapons by now but I was sweating bullets because of my weapon concealed and loaded in the cab.

This was towards the end of my second year in the business and I had bought a brand new, double cab, one ton Chevy pick up truck recently. If I was clever, I could be hiding the harvested plants in the double cab part of the truck, not in the back. As I went around to the passenger side with one officer and opened up the glove compartment to retrieve my registration, the other officer asked to look into the double cab area from the other side. Again, I said "yes", praying my gun was not laying in full view for him to see it. Then again I reasoned, as my mind raced on, maybe that would have been okay because I did have a permit to own it in my wallet. However, I knew

What I Learned In Life From A Liquid Manure Pit

full well in most states, it could not be loaded and within my reach, and I seriously doubted this state or county was any different.

As we finished up on the one side and shut the passenger side front door, the other officer opened the back door on the driver's side. Now I was sweating bullets even more, pardon the pun. He would have to see the gun any minute now. However, he soon closed the door, opened the driver's door, glanced in there and shut it too. Oh man, how had he missed the gun? Or, had he seen it and Indiana had a law to carry guns in vehicles? Well maybe a rifle hung in the window but not what I had in there totally concealed, and loaded for sure, within my reach! I am convinced that if the officer had seen that weapon, regardless of the county or state law's on these things, he would have asked to see my permit.

Later, after these officers left, when I was checking to see if I needed to go back to the motel and change my underwear, it appeared that when I slammed on my brakes, my gun, which was in its original cardboard box, had easily slid forwards, way up under the driver's seat. In fact, it was so snug, I had a hard time removing it. Of course, had they performed a thorough search, they would have found it but they were looking for a marijuana runner and it was obvious I was not doing anything of the sort. One officer had gone back to his vehicle and performed the perfunctory running of my plates, while I talked with the other officer. I began to recognize my voice again at the time.

I was settled down a lot now that my license cleared and now all three of us continued to talk as casual as one could imagine under the circumstances. Once they were convinced I had nothing to do with the earlier report, they began to talk even more freely about the problems in their county from hemp being grown there during WWII. I was truly interested and soaked it all in. Then I offered them a pop (not a brew), and asked them if they knew who had called the original report in? They told me where the call had come from. It was from a farm I had stopped at about a half hour ago and I had found no one home at the time.

Well, apparently, there was one person left behind and it was grandma. Having seen people cut hemp before and knowing everyone was gone to the big farm sale auction, she put two and two together, decided I was doing some kind of wrong, and the rest was history. I carried that adventure with me all over that county and those surrounding it. Since everyone but me knew about this hemp situation, it helped me to make more sales as I humbled myself more, and people enjoyed laughing at me and with me too. It is also one of my favorite stories to tell because it was exciting, to say the least, when it took place and I can still feel some of that excitement to this day, whenever I relive the story.

In sales, and in life, as you travel, it is usually a good thing to learn the local highlights and history of the area so you do not look totally stupid when confronted with pressing issues.

One time I was trying to find a farmer everyone told me was the man to call on. He supposedly loved tools and always had to have the latest and the best. Well, these kinds of guys are usually the busiest too. After hearing this for the third or fourth time, I asked for his farm to be noted on my plat book so I could at least start there and then continue to look for him as I made other calls. Well, this went off and on for a week and sometimes I missed him by minutes at home or at one of the places his hired help was working. A few times even his wife told me where to look for him, but I was not having any luck because he was constantly on the move.

CB's (Citizen Band radios for you youngsters reading this) were a good way to find people in farming country but you had to know what channel they used other than the one everyone used. By now I had to assume he knew I was looking for him and I know he heard me on the channel he used, because I would ask permission to "break" on the channel he used (a common courtesy in those days with CB people to interrupt others talking), but somebody else would give me permission to break instead of him. For some reason, the man everyone suggested I call on was impossible to pin down. Had I been set up? Was he a salesman hater? Of course, up to this point, I did not know and by now, after all the effort I had spent so far, I was not going to give up easily. Especially after realizing how big an operator he was.

It was going on three weeks now since I first heard about this guy, so I started making it a practice to hit his farm earlier and earlier. But to no avail. He was gone before the crack of dawn and I was becoming more and more frustrated. However, I just knew there was gold in them there hills if I kept mining. The only problem with this kind of callback strategy in the farm sales business was that I was working my way further out of his area everyday. So I tried to loop my call on him from the motel. For that reason, eventually I had to move to another motel in another city, so doubling back on him went from once a day in frequency to once or twice a week. Again, no luck.

Suddenly it dawned on me one day that I needed to try a totally different approach or I would be trying to catch this guy forever. He was definitely avoiding me and I did not know why. So, instead of revealing where I was, I listened to his chatter with his guys on the CB the next time I was in the area. And since I had been to all his staging areas more than once, I followed his progress on the plat book and finally figured out where he was headed next.

_While the popular definition of insanity was not around in those day, the concept certainly was__._ _"_**_If you continue to do the same things while expecting different results, you are insane._**_"_

When I arrived at that particular place, one of his hired hands I had heard earlier talking to him on the CB a few moments ago, greeted me. This was the second time I had met him so I said with a straight face… "I am meeting Terry here in a few moments. He is on his way here, right?" He nonchalantly said "Yep" and proceeded to go back to what he was doing before I had arrived. I quickly got my truck positioned in the shady area of the old shed and set up my wares on the tail gate, ready to go as soon as he arrived. I reasoned to myself that I had not just lied to his hired hand, I really was going to finally meet this guy.

Terry came rumbling down the lane and into the staging area. His pickup truck was a beauty and thank you Lord, it was a Chevy one-ton Silverado too. Being a one-ton model and the exact model I had (double cab also), except for the color, he and I had just discovered we had brother and sister vehicles. As he got out of his truck somewhat taken aback by that fact, I said… "I had heard my Chevy had a brother around these parts, and now I am seeing it with my own eyes." Don't ask me where that opening line came from but it was spontaneous and it worked. We talked a bit about our vehicles and we both had all the options. But I was careful not to lead in this discussion or try to "one up" him either. It was about a twenty-minute warm up and then I decided to segue into my sales pitch.

Honest to goodness, for some reason, up until now, he did not acknowledge who I was, even though I knew he knew. Finally, he broke the ice and said.... "So, I finally meet up with the guy who has been chasing me all over our county, trying to sell me some kind of nut and bolt and tool set up?" I decided I only had one answer and I gave it very enthusiastically.... "You bet I am and in my years of working this business all over the country, I've got to tell you that you have been the toughest guy to catch that I have ever chased." He responded grinning ear to ear and chuckling a bit.... "Well, I like to make salesmen earn their money and most give up long before you did. I figure if they have something that is that doggone important, they will keep trying until they find me." Man, was he right on that one. He was a huge farmer.

<u>Persistence and bugging a potential client have a fine line of difference between them. Cross over that line and you run the great risk of losing the sale altogether. However, the critical success factor is in disciplining yourself to keep on trying to land a qualified prospect</u>.

"Yes, I agree with you 100% on that one." I said wholeheartedly. "So being as you are the biggest farmer in the township, and maybe your county too, can I please quickly show you what I have?" He responded... "Make it quick, I need to be helping Tommy." Oh great I thought to myself, three weeks of chasing this guy only to be put on a tight time schedule. However, I pressed on with the demonstration since I already knew just about, as much of his farming operation now, as he and his help did, and I had little time for questions. That's when he did an amazing thing. Five minutes into the demonstration he said... "OK, I already know what you've got because I have seen your stuff everywhere lately. I am going to rig my pick up to carry both nut and bolt sets and I want one full set for my pole barn shop at my home too. I just cannot believe you are going to replace those drill bits free but I still need them anyway so give me a couple of the large sets."

What I Learned In Life From A Liquid Manure Pit

He continued as I tried to not show any unprofessional excitement like shouting... "All right!" or something like that. "I don't need anymore socket sets but I could use about six packets of hacksaw blades if they are any good, and a couple of easy out sets. Write up an invoice, put everything in my truck except the extra two bolt sets, and give me a total to sign when you are all done." I do not remember the final total of the order but it ranked right up there as one of my biggest single orders I ever had (not counting multiple sales at one stop like the one in Minnesota just a few days into my farm sales career).

That was it!!! After more than three weeks of chasing him, in less than 30 minutes I drove out of his staging area with this huge sale. He told me his wife would cut me a check when she saw his signature on the invoice when I delivered the extra nut and bolt sets to his home pole barn. Three weeks of chasing had culminated in a huge sale and he had given me another great story to tell, plus a phenomenal reference. Only I would have to wait to use the particulars of how I finally caught up with him starting a few counties away because, as you recall, this guy knew everyone in the area.

In addition, since I had totaled up his farming to be well over 2000 acres, he would need nut and bolt refills quite often. I did use his name to drop though, whenever I ran into a farmer who was farming 600 or more acres. Why? Because "Eagles fly with Eagles" and these guys wanted to be as big as him some day. To do that, they would have to be on top of the *cutting edge* of things he was doing and emulate him as much as possible, even if they envied him or disliked him. However, as time passed, I learned, he really was a likable guy once I met him, and everyone respected him. My sources proved correct too when they told me this program would be "right up his alley" and he would buy once I got to see him.

If you have a good product and/or service, and you have the persistence and courage to get your message out there, you will find the word gets around allowing you to parlay the so-called "bandwagon" approach to your favor.

Chapter 13

You Need To Find A Farmer Friend And A Banker Friend In The Township You Plan To Work

One rainy day, while working in an area that was mostly grain farmers, I lucked into a situation that would dramatically change my pattern of working a township. My second call was on a fairly good-sized farmer. He was farming over 1000 acres and he did not have any livestock. When we got to talking, he seemed to know everyone, especially those I "named dropped" on sales I had already made. After he bought the whole nine yards, he started asking me if I had called on "such in such" or "so and so". I had just begun working in this area of the county and obviously, every new name he came up with I had not called on. He looked at me and said... "My son farms a couple of townships over, about twenty miles away. If I ride with you today and help you sell a few of these nut and bolt kits and some of your tools too, will you give me a set of long and short bolts free for my son?"

Careful name-dropping in sales can make you a lot of money, as long as the person you are currently selling to has no problem with those names you are name-dropping. And occasionally, a great new idea to make more sales is laid in your lap and you need to be ready to make a "go or no go" decision, immediately.

I did not hesitate for a moment. I knew exactly what that set of free nut and bolt kits would cost me and how little in total gross sales it would take to break even. From then on, it would be the "gravy train" for me and so I said with great enthusiasm… "We have a deal, let's go". We headed into the house, he grabbed a thermos of coffee and two cups, and off we went. By now, the rain was settling into what farmers call "a three day rain". Instead of a cloud burst or two that might be so scattered that they miss certain areas altogether, this was a very wide spread weather front delivering light, soft, drenching rain that gave crops exactly what they needed to grow intensely for the next two to three weeks or so. These grain farmers would already be in a good mood because this slow, steady rain was coming at a perfect time to boost their final yields of corn and beans, bushels per acre.

We passed the next farm and he told me "not to bother with him". However, the next farm on that road he motioned me to pull in and it looked, neat, clean, and very organized at first glance. The reliable sign of a pickup truck next to the house, was a sure sign this farmer was home. We pulled in and he told me to honk the horn (something I rarely if ever did unless there was a definite reason to do so). He jumped out and approached the backdoor. I got out and from this moment on, I began to discover this man I was driving around with, knew virtually every good farmer I should be working with in this county. They respected him fully (unless they resented his success). He knocked on the backdoor and immediately the farmer we were calling on came out shaking his hand and asking him… "what are you doing here today?"

He pointed to me and said… "I met this guy earlier today and his program is so good, I wanted everyone I knew to know about it before he moved on. Can we pull into your shed Tim and get out of

What I Learned In Life From A Liquid Manure Pit

the rain?" I must admit dollar signs started rolling in my eyes. It was just like the moment back in Minnesota when I backed into that pole barn on that stormy night in Minnesota, and saw all those farmers, and heard the owner of the farm tell everyone I was the guy who saved his cow and calf earlier that day.

No sale had been consummated just yet, but third party sales, especially from people highly respected like this man who was riding with me, was guaranteed money in the bank. In addition, to take this third party referral to the ultimate level, not only was he riding with me, he was telling farmers in the area, first hand, why they should buy from me! I pulled into the shed to get out of the rain and talk a little bit more, and in less than twenty minutes, the sale was completed and we were on our way again to another farm.

That day we had a 1000 percent batting average which myself and other salespeople in the company had done before, but rarely. The volume of sales was awesome but we talked a lot at each farm so it was not a record breaker. Everyone bought something and it wasn't just a token purchase. I knew if we kept on going at this pace, I would be out of material by Wednesday, maybe earlier. As the day ended, as I said earlier, I had not broken a one-day sales record for me or for the company, but I had come very close I discovered later. Towards the end of the day, I suggested we head to his son's farm and he said… "We can do that tomorrow or Wednesday." I said… "Okay, but at the rate you and I are going, I don't want to run out of the kits I promised you I would give him." He acquiesced and I took a hard right turn and headed East.

After meeting his son who was just like his father, and realizing he was probably almost as influential, especially to the younger generation of farmers, I suggested to him that when I got in his area, if he would ride with me some rainy day, I would do the same for a friend of his, just as his father and I had done for him. He said… "That's a deal; I will come up with someone. In fact, come to think of it, I have just the guy in mind." Immediately I not only gave him the two bolt sets free, but I threw in a large drill bit set in the process too. I began to think maybe I had fallen into a sales concept that would completely change the way I operated in a county.

What I Learned In Life From A Liquid Manure Pit

Because this concept proved to be so successful, as time progressed, whenever I found a well liked and respected big farmer, I would try to institute this program with him. The only catch was it did require him riding with me and it was usually on a rainy day. Sometimes in a new county, through one method or another, I asked about who this type of guy might be and where he farmed. Then I would head directly to him and make the same offer. It was a hard deal to turn down if they were a progressive farmer.

In other situations, since in bigger counties I would set up a temporary bank account in a town, I would occasionally talk to a banker as I opened that account with a couple of thousand dollars in cash (keep in mind, that money was deposited but soon, very little was left in the account as I finished in the county and moved on—it was just a convenience to me to have the account so I could cash checks and get lots of cash and checks out of the cab of my pickup). Eventually I would use this tactic with bankers more and more to take the guesswork out of the deal of who I wanted to seek out. And of course, it cut down on my search time too. Bankers were a lot more cautious in giving out information but I always asked it as I was opening up that new account with them.

__Always be looking for ways to improve on a great idea because when you do, eventually a better, more effective way of doing something will develop.__

In sales, word of mouth and third party advertising is fantastic and it makes your job a whole lot easier. For that reason, I honed this tactic to a scientific, template approach. In addition, along the way I developed some finesses tactics I must admit I learned by accident. One of them that Bob, the owner of the company had taught me, was very powerful. It was the shirt pocket stuffed with invoices I mentioned earlier in my book. Later on, after I left the company, I heard Bob had developed a way to work with 4H and Future Farmer's of America groups for fund raising and to be able to get to these good farmers in each county, quite easily.

I realized one day early in this farm sales business that the eye contact of the farmer would definitely be drawn to staring at my shirt pocket when it was bulging with invoices. After observing that a few more times after trying it in Minnesota and realizing, I had been asked more than once... "So who yah been selling to in my area?" I would always start out the day with my shirt pocket stuffed to the hilt with invoices. It made an obvious impact and statement that people were buying what I had to sell. The only drawback to this tactic was that my shirt pockets tended to rip on one side or the other so I needed to keep my pockets reasonably full, and I kept the other invoices in the truck when the question came up. I loved saying... "Besides these, I have a lot more in the cab of my truck. Do you want to see them too?" Interestingly enough, while those extra invoices were there, I never once had a taker on that question.

People who are already winners or are "wannabe winners", do not want to be left out when something good is happening around them. In sales, we call that the "bandwagon" effect and I learned to utilize this tactic to the fullest. Existing clients have jumped on the bandwagon in the parade and potential clients want to be on the bandwagon too. By namedropping and having sales receipts readily available, the parade with more and more bandwagons, keeps getting longer and longer.

Another tactic I developed that was a spin off of these proven tactics would be when, for one reason or another, I became very good friends with a new farmer, regardless if he bought from me or not. They didn't have to be the biggest or the best farmer in the county, he just had to be the most likeable and most trustworthy from the moment I met him. I always asked bankers about that particular farmer. If I was sure of that after we met, I would come right out and ask him for his help in narrowing down the farmers I should definitely call on in his county, especially his township. And I always promised never to reveal my source unless they gave their okay to me to do so. If they bought first, this tactic worked over 90% of the time. If they did not buy much, it was a little harder, but I still tried it.

Again, these guys did not have to be as guarded as bankers were and I rarely had one of them turn me down when I asked. Once the plat book was marked and valuable information had been gained, I would ask permission to reward him for what he had just done for me. Believe it or not, sometimes these types would turn me down on the reward offer. At that point, I could easily tell who would be insulted if I insisted on the reward again, and who would not.

Continuous Improvement in everything we do is the name of the game if you want to be the best you can be. In sales, it is a Critical Success Factor and never an option.

Sometimes I would use an old but proven sales tactic called *feel, felt, found* and occasionally one called a *reverse sell* approach too. The feel, felt, found one worked like this. If I sensed any hesitation and I was hit with a strong objection (which by the way, I think of as "buying signals" today instead of objections), I would totally agree with them and let them know I fully understood how they were *feeling* because I had called on hundreds of farmers before them who had *felt* that same, exact way at this point in my presentation too. Then I would go on to say…. "But you know what? Here is what they *found* when they finally decided to go with us. They loved the program and told many of their friends about us. So with that in mind, what would be the harm in trying our program for a year?"

That is when I would shut up and wait for a response. Hell could freeze over before I would talk, so the decision was placed on the farmer and he would have to say something next. I was not about to speak first and talk my way out of the sale. Shutting up after you ask a closing question can be an extremely hard tactic to learn, but it makes sales people a fortune when they master it.

Reverse selling was when farmers seemed to keep giving me objections and it appeared I might lose the entire sale. At that point, I might say something to the effect of… "You know, I think you convinced me, maybe you are right. Maybe this program is not right for you. I have sold to many farmers around here and around the country who love this program because they farm a few hundred acres up to a 1000 or more. I can see where this might be to big an investment for your size of operation. Then I would stare at the nut and bolt kit, never at them, and stay quiet.

That is when they usually asked me curtly… "What kind of acreage do you think I am farming anyway?" I would claim ignorance even if I had totaled it up in the plat book earlier. Usually one thing led to another and they began convincing me and selling me that they could use the program too. More often than not, eventually a nice sale of some kind developed. And you know what? I never considered this a trick. I truly believed in what products and services we were offering and I felt it was my duty to hang in there with a qualified, potential customer until they convinced themselves to buy it.

__If you really believe in what you are selling, and you honestly know your customer will love what you have for them, once they go with your program, it is OK to use sales tactics that finesse you into a sale.__

Chapter 14

Futures, Hog Bellies And Being Talked Into Something I Knew Absolutely Nothing About

―――

As the weeks went by, then months and finally a couple of years in this business, I felt I had become a seasoned farm sales person expert, and quite frankly, I really did know my way around different types of farms, all over this country. Nevertheless, there was always something new to learn, and sometimes those lessons were more painful than others.

One day, while dealing with a very large grain farmer, who had taken an instant liking to me (and vice versa), he said to me... "Are you in the market right now on beans and corn?" I did not want to look stupid but I did not want to lie either so I said... "No I am not right now, should I be?" That was all it took. He instantly said... "We are going to have a shortage of beans this year and if you've got $5000 to $10,000 cash laying around that you can spare, you can

What I Learned In Life From A Liquid Manure Pit

double that or triple it in the next few months, guaranteed, and I will help you do it. Yah interested?" Oh boy, I never heard of this scam before now and wondered what the catch was.

The funny thing is, while I was making tons of money in this business, I constantly had to buy new inventory for my salespeople and me now that I was a distributor. Therefore, I did not have an easy five grand to lay my hands on but if I did a little "robbing Peter to pay Paul" and moved some money around, I could come up with the five grand and turn it over to him. He made it easy for me to do too, and to this day, knowing he really had nothing to gain but a break-even in doing this for me, I do not know exactly why he chose to do it. He had his wife type up a legal IOU piece of paper and when I saw him the following week, I gave him the cash (after juggling some funds around) and we each had copies of that paper. It plainly stated that on paper, I owned over a thousand bushels of his soybeans now.

In effect, he had tens of thousands of bushels of soybeans he was sitting on and they were rising in market price daily. I was not family, just a salesperson friend he took an instant liking to. In addition, he was so successful looking, I trusted him instantly too, even if it just seemed to easy to be true (that's a big hint on what is to come later). For some reason, he gave me the impression with his big, beautiful, impressive farm with all the trimmings, that he had done this kind of thing before and won. I had already learned about how farmers, who could afford it, would "sit" on corn and beans until they reached a market price they liked instead of selling when everyone else did at harvest time. This guy told me…. "I am not pressured like other farmers who have to sell. I can sit on these beans as long as I want to and now you own a small but valuable part of them."

This guy was the biggest farmer in the county and a banker had directed me to him originally as a great prospect. In addition, since he liked me and wanted to help me, he gave me all the inside information on how I would double my money overnight, if not triple it. Here is what was taking place as I recall. There were a number of things happening across the country, including some heavy drought areas and some washed out areas. That resulted in late spring planting of beans that would severely cut the total bushel output when harvested. Then too, apparently we were selling grain overseas in a big way. Therefore, he told me the price of beans would go from around the current price of $4.40 a bushel to $11.00 or even $12.00 a bushel! Previously I had seen some major price fluctuations in the farm markets, but nothing like this one promised to be.

As best I can remember, I got in at around $4.40 a bushel, paid directly to him, even though they really were his beans I was buying. Now that I was officially in the business of owning a little over 1,100 bushels of beans, I tuned into the farm report each day. Sure enough, he was right; those beans just kept going up "the limit" each day. Farmers around the country who still had beans were very happy and our company's total sales reflected this happiness. My farmer was riding on tens of thousands of bushels so he had a lot to gain or lose and I trusted his judgment. However, once my money had more than doubled, I called him and asked if I should cash out with him. "Absolutely not!" He replied…. "When we get in the $11.00 a bushel range, then I will start making a 'sell' decision." "Well"… I thought to myself, "He has been right on this so far, and he was the obvious expert who played this game often, so why should I worry now?"

There ain't no free lunch and anytime something seems too good to be true, it is time to have some 'due diligence' performed before you get in too deep.

Since, he was the expert and I was totally new to this game, while I wanted to call him many times and cash out with him, I did not call again until I heard soybeans had hit $11.00 a bushel. After all, he promised me he would sell at that price and he predicted it would happen and it had! Now I called and really did want to at least sell my share of beans so I could make some great money. This $11.00 a bushel price was an unheard of record that had never before happened. I have heard this record high has been hit since but it was the talk of every stop I made, and of course, I let each farmer know I was in the market too… "In a big way."

Then, before that day was half over, something changed that upset the entire applecart and sent chills down my spine and pains into my butt where I kept my wallet. Nationally the government made some moves and some kind of ban or severe restriction on exporting was announced because of the way this highly inflated price per bushel of beans (and to some extent corn too) had started to have a ripple negative effect on feed directly and food products indirectly. To some extent, it is a lot like what is happening with Ethanol fuel plants today now that more and more corn and beans are going into the production of Ethanol. Well anyway, beans began to "drop the limit" or as I recall, 20 cents a bushel each day. I quickly found out with my next phone call that when that takes place, you could not sell in that kind of crash condition, until the market stabilized, because buyers wanted to see how low beans would go. Oh boy, that was news to me. What was I going to go to school on next?

At $8.00 a bushel, it was still apparent I would come out very well on my initial investment. However, the price of beans just kept dropping the limit each day. At $6.00 a bushel, I began to panic and made yet another call. "I think beans will level out at around $5.50 a bushel and then I will sell it all."....he said. Well, it never did. In fact, when it was all over, beans had dropped to around $3.20 a bushel! I do not know when he finally sold all his beans because remember, he did not have to sell.

I lost around fifteen hundred dollars (which is a lot of money now but it was *really* a lot of money back then). When I swung back to his farm, he felt really bad but he also wanted me to know just how much he had lost (on paper mind you, not real dollars like I had) "thanks to the government sticking its nose in where it shouldn't have." Then he mentioned he was sure they would go back up so if I wanted to "let it ride", he would hold on to my portion of the beans. Not on your life I thought. I took a check from him and cashed it at the local bank and it cleared with no problem. Once again, I had added another painful learning experience to my farm sales career. The only good news out of all this was the fact that I did not come across this farmer when beans were much higher a bushel. I could have lost my entire original investment in that case. You could argue he made money on me because beans did go up a bit as the year progressed, but never above that starting price of $4.40 a bushel.

<u>Life is a compilation of learning experiences where you win some and you lose some. I have made so doggone many mistakes in my life, I work hard on not making the same one twice. That really is the name of the game.</u>

Chapter 15

Wild Times Following Up Farm Machinery Show Leads In The Rural Parts Of Kentucky And Tennessee

O ne of the interesting parts of selling to farmers was when, as a company, we would bring in distributors and salespeople from around the country to work the National Farm Machinery Show, held those days in Louisville Kentucky. It was always held in the winter before farmers actually started planting in most parts of the country. I swear this show would run for eight to ten days but it probably was more like five to seven. During that period of time, thousands upon thousands of farmers from all over the country, and ranchers from out West, would parade past our booth where we demonstrated our wares along with thousands of other companies.

Many times, you would meet one of your existing customers and have some catching up to do while making sure you were not

What I Learned In Life From A Liquid Manure Pit

letting a "live one" walk by the booth in the meantime. When that happened, I would attempt to use my highly satisfied customer help me convince the potential customer standing at our booth, that this was a great idea to buy into and have on their farm. This show was exhausting and by the end of each day, the team working at the time was ready to unwind. But that's another group of stories with some funny twists that I can tell you if I ever meet you in person.

Back then, the rules of the show stated you were not allowed to sell anything off the floor and if you were caught, the penalty was severe. Therefore, if you wanted to cut a deal with someone, and not have to hunt them down somewhere across America, you arranged to meet them at a certain place and at a certain time, or in the parking lot. You usually offered some kind of discount because if you could make this quick, low overhead sale, you came way out ahead because you did not have to run them down later, or risk the chance they changed their mind. The only catch on the instant sales was they had to have driven to the show. Most people however, wanted you to deliver to their farm.

Moreover, there was another factor figured into the picture. By now, we had very active competition throughout much of the country. Therefore, many times the farmer would stop at two or three similar booths and write up the same order. They did this when they really wanted something because they had experienced at this show before, where they would ask for sales people to call on them, many times a salesperson would never show up. Therefore, by being the salesperson that got to the farmer first during or after the show, you were 95% guaranteed to close the deal, if they really did want the product and had not changed their mind and gotten cold feet in the meantime.

After a couple of these shows, our sales team got smarter and smarter. Instead of waiting after the show to divide up leads, we would let a salesperson go with a cluster of leads in a particular area or grouping of bordering states, where we did not have a distributor. In this way, we would beat the competition cold because those same farmers and ranchers were most likely stopping at the competition's booths too. So the sales leads were developing in a systematic, chronological order we could get a jump on, with an early start out the gate.

One of the fascinating things about sales is when you are constantly working on ways to outsmart the competition, and being ahead of them. When you focus on this, you become more and more effective and profitable.

I always volunteered for the obscure leads that were good potential sales, but harder to get to in the not so populated places. I had discovered early these were almost 100% done deals because of two things: the competition did not want to take the time to find them and since they were off the beaten path, they did not want to go way out of their way with the chance of possibly not getting a sale.

Because we would invariably run down leads written up by other salespeople, all of us working the booths made sure we clearly printed phone numbers on those invoice copies and we also made sure we carefully jotted down some basic directions on the back, if the farmer or rancher was not easy to find. 9 times out of 10, this system worked well. However, sometimes it failed miserably because one little detail was left out from the directions, or the phone number was wrong, or we just did not get them noted correctly on the back of the invoice, in the first place. One time we had a dyslexic salesperson work the booth. Back then we did not even know the term but we knew the results. Half the orders he wrote up had transposed phone numbers just for starters!

One year I volunteered to take the leads in the backwoods country of Kentucky and Tennessee. The total sales potential on the leads I got were excellent and I had fairly good directions on all of them. In addition, there was a phone number on each one too. My first stops were like shooting fish in the barrel and the farmers were shocked that I was so close on their heels from them attending the show and returning home. One farmer had literally gotten home two hours before I called him and then showed up.

You had to rely heavily on your fellow salespeople working the tradeshow booth to get those phone numbers and directions correctly or that lead might be lost forever, or at least until we saw them again next year at the show and they were mad at us for not following up with them. Because these were not the territories of regular distributors, we did not have the old reliable plat maps to guide us. Instead, we had maps of the state, those basic directions, and a phone number we hoped was accurate.

One day on this above trip, I was in the middle of nowhere, in a wilderness area in Tennessee. At the last town with a pay phone, I tried the farmer one more time because the directions, which another salesperson had taken, were not clear. Again, the phone rang and rang so I decided to give it a shot and stay with the directions, the way I interpreted them. Normally that was not a wise thing to do in this part of the country because one wrong turn could get you into a situation where you would have to backtrack for miles.

Just when I was about to give up and was thoroughly lost, another amazing story started to unfold in my farm sales career. I was using the Atlas I had and the hand drawn map on the invoice, along with my trusty compass mounted on the window of my truck. Combined, these tools usually guided me to my target destination. In this particular situation, the last few miles of frustration brought me upon a farm right out of the movie Deliverance. I swear I heard the music of that most recent 1972 movie playing somewhere in the background. As I mentioned earlier, I did carry a 357-magnum gun loaded for protection so when I pulled into this place, I felt behind the seat to make sure my gun was in easy reach if I needed it, and it was.

This farm was a total mess. There were farm machinery elements in all stages of repair (or should I say disrepair) lying all over the place. Pigs and chickens were running around freely as were cats and dogs. The dogs were coonhounds baying very mournfully while wagging their tails as they came up to me. So, I figured their bark was far louder than their bite. When I talked to the loudest one as I got out of the truck, he came to me wagging his tail harder now as if we were long lost friends. Now I have got to tell you, this poor dog had more ticks on him than fur at first glance.

Sometimes in life, there are so many negative signals and red flags, we need to really stop and carefully listen more closely to what they are telling us.

The other dog was a little more skittish and stayed back. The house looked like it had been built out of a combination of wood, tin

What I Learned In Life From A Liquid Manure Pit

and tarpaper and I had no idea how it could still be standing. There was no screen door and the front door was wide open. There were no kids to be seen. I wondered if in fact, he was not farming anymore at all. About this time an old codger in at least his late seventies, came out of the inside of the place saying nothing and he was a sight to behold, and he fit right into the surroundings. Leaning next to the front door was an old over, under, double-barreled shotgun like my Grandpa Hale used to have. I think it was of the 12 gauge variety.

I would always call my wife when I went into these backwoods areas, to let her know where I was going that day and where I hoped to end up. In that way, if I did disappear off the face of the earth, at least they would have a starting point to begin looking for me. Feeling a little uneasy, I made sure I was not too far away from my open cab door and my gun. As the dogs sniffed and peed on my tires, this old man, who was not much for talk, spoke up and he wanted to know "What the Sam Hill you doing on my land, Boy?" Now with the stories I had heard about moonshiners and how they treated outsiders if they stumbled upon a still, I kept my distance and actually looked around to make sure there was no one else coming up from behind me, to catch me by surprise. Therefore, to be safe, and have ready access to my pistol, I kept my driver door open and I did not stray far from the truck.

I told him I was looking for a particular farmer by name and my directions had led me to his place. So I wasn't sure if I was totally lost or just a few miles from this guy. With tobacco juice running out of both sides of his mouth, he grinned a wicked kind of smile with no teeth and said in a strange, incoherent way that he knew him and he could give me a shortcut to reach him about ten miles from where we stood. He took a stick and drew a map in the dirt. I told him I understood it and off I went, being careful not to run over any of his prized animals on my way out.

Well, the first part of the trip was a couple of miles of backtracking down his road. Then I headed due South down a two track road that continued to get narrower and narrower. Soon tree branches were hitting my rearview mirrors and I was beginning to think I might have made a wrong turn. However, there was no backing up now and my trusty compass said I was continuing to head due south, and that was where I wanted to go, or so I thought. Suddenly I came upon a little clearing that seemed to be big enough to do a turn around, if you jockeyed back and fourth a few times. It was then that I saw a creek in front of me that was about 20 feet wide, with crystal clear water, and flowing fairly well. On the other side of the creek was a white post with crudely painted black letters clearly showing the depth of the water in feet.

What I was dealing with was called a "creek bridge". These concrete squares the width of the creek were built during the Great Depression by the "CC" boys (Conservation Corps). So, instead of incurring the expense of building a bridge, that might get washed out anyway during a flood, they built these creek bridges, which under normal water levels, kept you from sinking into the mud when you crossed. The water gauge warned you from getting into water too deep to drive through. That was the reason for the turn around on both sides of the creek. The gauge looked to read a little over a foot and having gone over this type of bridge before at that depth or even a little deeper, I knew my one-ton pickup truck, which sat up fairly high, would be high enough to keep from being flooded, especially since there would be solid concrete underneath me.

When you are in someone else's backyard or sales territory, you had better keep your wits about you at all times or you could lose more than the sale.

I took one more look at the water depth gauge pole and proceeded to slowly and carefully cross the water, making sure not to slip off the creek bridge. It did not take more than a few seconds after I was half way across that creek to know I was in big trouble. The water was much deeper than the gauge read and I realized I was into some muck too. With the weight of the truck and lots of materials to boot, and the mud and sand bottom, I was stuck fast because my nice truck was not equipped with four-wheel drive.

I had a little trouble opening my door because the water was above the running board and making a nice pressure wave on it. With all the weight on the truck, I wasn't too worried about the truck and materials floating away, and the materials would remain high and dry based on the depth of water I was in. However, here I was, stuck hard fast in the back hills of Tennessee with no triple AAA

What I Learned In Life From A Liquid Manure Pit

to call to pull me out. Suddenly my heart skipped a beat! As I was getting out of the truck and carefully stepping into the creek so as not to fall, there on the other side of the creek, about thirty feet up the road, was the old guy I had met not more than twenty minutes ago, sitting on a small Massey Ferguson tractor, smiling that toothless smile once again!

"Yah all stuck?"….. he shouted with a definite sadistic overtone to it. "Yeah I'm stuck, probably right up to the axles. Can you help tow me out?" He smiled and said… "Sure can, but it will cost you $50." Now folks, in the early seventies, $50 was a lot more money than $50 is worth today. In addition, I realized instantly I had been set up and screwed over by this old guy who most likely made a decent living off of dumb, trusting people like me. To make matters worse, he did not help one bit. I went to him and he handed me the hook attached to the cable and power take off wench on his tractor. He asked for the $50 right then and there and I reluctantly paid it to him.

I was furious, but I was also helpless and I needed to get that expensive truck loaded down with that valuable cargo, out of the mud, and get me on the way again, regardless of where I was or what it cost. To add insult to injury, I had to go under water a few times to try and get the cable hooked up to the front frame of the truck. I had done that type of thing before, but never under water. Once I finally accomplished that deed, which was very tricky because I wore contacts and had to squint so as not to wash them out of my eyes, he revved up his tractor and power take off. Slowly but surely, he pulled me out of the creek and into the turn around clearing on the other side of the creek. At one point in this operation, because the combined weight of my one ton pickup truck and thousands of pounds of material in the back, it almost started pulling him and his tractor towards the creek.

Honest to goodness, I was half tempted to pull my gun out and take that $50 back. However, I also reasoned that if I did, that kind of thing would not get me anywhere in the end, and I might end up dead in the process, not knowing exactly where I was or maybe who was watching. Therefore, I swallowed my pride, accepted my fate, and continued south as planned.

What I Learned In Life From A Liquid Manure Pit

To my amazement, not ten minutes more, as the road got wider, I came to a tar or paved road. By then I was able to figure out how to find the farmer I had been searching for all along. My luck started to turn for the better then as my elusive farmer was home and he bought everything he said he wanted at the show, and then some. Eventually I asked him if he knew about the guy who took me for the $50 and he laughed a hard laugh and said he sure did, and that this old guy had been doing that same trick for as many years as he could remember!

He then went on to explain that the directions he gave the salesperson he talked to at the show should not have brought me that way. I had taken the wrong direction at a fork in the road, twenty miles back, on the other side of the creek, which would have taken me over a real bridge that crossed that infamous creek. Oh well, it was another learning experience and quite frankly, I was glad to be alive.

There were a couple of other times in the deep South were I could feel the hair raising on the back of my neck as I pulled into a place. One time the situation looked so bad, I stopped in the drive as I was approaching the house, since it was the end of the road like the other farm I just told you about. I proceeded to back down the drive very quickly in a straight line. You got real good at backing up in this business because the need to do so happened all the time. The secret was to never make a sudden move with the steering wheel, just tiny increment turns, or you would end up in a ditch or worse.

Well, since this place looked worse than the other one I just told you about, while I was backing up, I saw these two surly looking guys come out of the house, if you could call it a house, and one was carrying a shotgun under his arm! I never did find out what was going on there and I never will. But this was one time I really listened to the red flags. I half expected to be shot at but they just stared at me as I continued to back towards an area almost a quarter of a mile away where I could safely turn around. Once again, I was way off the beaten path and lost and the road ended to my surprise, right in these people's front yard like the other farmer. In those days, either those signs that warned you there was "No Outlet" were torn down, or they were never put up in the first place. Of course, stories and rumors about people like me disappearing in these places, never to be seen or heard of again, were always in the back of my mind.

One time in late August when the corn was at its peak in height and maturity of between seven to eight feet or more, I was lost and trying to find a cross road or something that would help me get my bearings and then sync up my plat book with where I actually was located. I had the radio playing with country music, I had my head buried in my plat book wondering why it was not making any sense, and I was rolling west on a dirt road at a slow rate of speed.

To make matter worse, as I mentioned, since the corn was as high as it was going to get, I could not see in any direction except in front of me and behind me. It has always amazed me how you can drive many miles on a highway and suddenly realize you arrived in a certain area without really paying attention to your trip along the way. In this case, that was happening to me when suddenly, I felt my truck rise up a slight grade I had not noticed until now.

The minute you get too comfortable and relaxed, and take your mind off of what is taking place, you could be in a world of hurt instantly.

That got my attention quickly and I suddenly realized I was going up to the top of a very rural railroad crossing with no warning lights. I guess in those days they figured you could easily see trains coming and going in that flat land. Plus, the train track was elevated. That was except for a month or so before the corn was harvested. As I said earlier, there was no flashing lights, just wooden railroad crossing signs on each side of the tracks. I had barely cleared the last row of corn before I started up the elevated railroad track crossing, so I was totally committed to crossing over to the other side. It was at that exact moment I realized a train was bearing down on me not more than 100 feet away with the horn blaring above the sound of my radio, and the headlight beaming right into the pupils of my wide opened eyes!

I really had no time to react and my adrenaline, while surging now, did not know exactly where to surge to in my body, except maybe in the vicinity of my underwear. Thank God the momentum of my truck carried me over the crossing just in the nick of time! That train passed so close to my rear bumper, it moved my entire truck with its envelope of rushing wind. I did floor my truck for a few seconds but I was already out of harm's way because my truck's initial momentum was what had saved my life originally.

Once safe, I came to a quick halt and sat there shaking and basically in a state of shock. I could hear the train engineer blasting the horn solid now, definitely expressing anger that I had been so stupid and come so close to messing up his day. Then, after thanking the good Lord for sparing my life once again, and after being upset with my own stupidity, I started to play some mind games. Since that train had missed obliterating my truck and me by only two seconds at the most, I wondered about those few seconds earlier in my day where I could have been delayed just a little longer.

What if I had taken a few more seconds at my last stop? What if I had taken just a few more seconds at the gas station filling up this morning? I came up with an unending list of "what if" thoughts that could have placed me right in front of that train and sure death. I reasoned later that God must have had more in store for me to accomplish in life. Now today, having had a number of these types of close calls in my life, I can see the many things He has had me do, and the many lives I have touched in a positive way. I can fully understand why these close calls in my farming sales career did not end with my life being terminated back then.

You can get so lost in what you are trying to accomplish, that you run the chance of missing your mark altogether. In the old days, they called that "So close to the forest, you cannot see the trees".

Chapter 16

Silos, Equipment, Barns And Home-Judging Are Not All They Appear To Be

As I mentioned earlier in this book, one of the first sales jobs I had where I relied totally on a sales commission for income, was when I was selling Fuller Brush products door-to-door. That year was an exceptionally hot and humid summer in my home town of St. Louis, Missouri. Like most of my old football buddies from high school, I went looking for a good paying construction job that would make me some excellent cash between getting out of college for the summer, and going back to college in the fall. However, I was not lucky enough to land a construction job since, they were very scarce that year.

I had to look for something else in the classified Want Ads and when I saw an ad that said… "Make as much money as you want. We will train you. $100.00 per week up to $200.00 is possible in just one week's time." Well it was worth looking into. When I showed up for the interview, there seemed to be a few hundred other people who read the ad and had the same idea.

I showed up at a large, very nice looking home in a well to do part of our city. The interviews were being processed very quickly, despite the huge number of people who showed up. Somehow, the interviewers were able to quickly sort out who they thought might make it, and who would not. I was selected as one that would move to the next step and I was told I would need to come back for classroom training the next day, all day, and then, the following day I would work in the field with one of the field trainers for a half day. Next, if that worked out, I would be on my own and they said, if I worked hard and followed the training, I would be making great money that second afternoon and everyday I wanted to work (except Sunday), from then on.

The training went well and a few of us faster learners got to go out with a trainer that afternoon, hopefully not having to wait another day to start making money. They had taught me a proven template that worked. Briefly, it worked like this. I carried a kit full of items they supplied me, and I carried refills in my car. I was assigned an area to work all the homes on both sides of each city block. They instructed you to park your car in the middle of the block and then begin your sales path up one half of the block, cross over to the other side, work the entire block on the other side passing by your car to stock up on items you needed refilling.

Your sales approach and tactic was simple too. You walked up the steps to the front porch, sat your sales kit down, rang the doorbell or knocked on the door and waited for someone to come to the door. The luxury of air-conditioning in the area I was working in was yet to be an affordable, normal thing, so everyone's door and windows were wide open (and you must remember, this was in the early 1960's and it was an entirely different world).

When the housewife arrived at the screen door, I had been trained to say... "Hello mam, my name is Stan Barnes and I am working to make money for college. But before I say anymore, is it possible to get a glass of water?" Nine times out of ten they invited you into the kitchen (again, remember this was almost 50 years ago). Once you were in the kitchen and received the glass of water, sometimes with ice, you drank it politely but you really gulped those first swallows as if you needed it and you said "Thank you so much mam." I had great bladder holding power in those days and you obviously needed it with all that drinking of water.

We were trained to also make sure our sales kit was near us and preferably elevated on a kitchen counter or table so you did not have to bend over to open it when it was time to show your wares. After those couple of swallows, it was time to move into the sales presentation. "Mam, I have quite an array of products in my sales kit you might be interested in. Is it okay if I show you some while I finish my glass of water?"

I do not remember ever getting a "no" at this point, if I got inside the home. Virtually all of the time you sold something, even if it was just an inexpensive item. They also taught me the valuable "add on" tactic once you sold the main concept of buying something in this door-to-door, instant delivery, sales process. Plus, they taught me to watch for excitement or emotions of the housewife and key in on that. Only much later in my life would I realize the great things they taught me in such a short period of time. I was so pleased about how the system continued to work again and again. However, there were a few times when it did not because they did not let me in the house or denied me the glass of water. Or, they told me at the screen door they were not interested in whatever I was selling. And of course, some people were not home.

Whatever you are selling, the customer buys emotionally first and logically second with very few exceptions. In addition, you need to start with your best products and services, not your worst or the lowest cost ones. The reason is simple, if starting at the top does not work, you can always ease the customer down to a lesser value product or service. There are a few exception to this rule (i.e. the old "bait and switch" tactic or lead item, or selling from the bottom up instead of the top down), but most of the time you need to start with your best, at the top.

Well, the first week I was amazed at my efforts. I made $107.00 clear and to me that was a lot of money. In fact, it was almost twice as much as my buddies were making while sweating out there in that hot sun doing construction work. The next week I cleared $121.00 and the man heading up that division told me... "Stan, if you stick with this, you could make a small fortune this summer. Right now, you just set a record for this years two week gross sales total in the St. Louis area for new salespeople." Man, I was pumped after he told me that. Then something strange started happening the third week. I got smart, or so I thought.

That third Monday as I went to work, I started thinking about how I could do this even smarter and not work so hard. Part of my thinking was to figure out ahead of time who those people were who were going to reject me and who those housewives were that were going to buy or not. After all, I had two record sales weeks under my belt and I was invincible in this door-to-door sales game. I started "curb judging" the homes and I tried to guess from experience which homes those rejection types of people lived in so I could walk by them and not waste my time with them (it is called "curb judging" in sales and it is a universal term because door-to-door salesmen and regular salesmen would get in trouble when they started looking at a home or business and deciding from the appearance only, if they were a good prospect or not).

The next Cardinal Sin I did in sales, was to break the proven sales template further by not asking for the glass of water because I hated having to take time out to relieve myself that often. A funny thing started happening right away that Monday morning. I did not get into those kitchens as easily and sales were getting tougher and tougher. Rejection at the front door started to increase. Then I really broke the template when I quit carrying my heavy sales kit up those concrete stairways, up to the porch door (that was the weirdest change from the template of all—I must have figured if they were interested, I could run and get it).

By Wednesday noon, I had only cleared about $25.00 and rejection was running very high. I blamed everything for my lack of sales on something other than me. It was the neighborhood, the heat, you name it, but not me. By the end of the day, I quit and and headed home and told my parents and wife.... "If my boss calls, tell him I got another job and would be bringing the supplies I had left in inventory assigned to me, and the money from my sales, over to

What I Learned In Life From A Liquid Manure Pit

his home tomorrow." I did not want to face him at all because I had come to actually dread sales almost instantly.

I have looked back on that job many times over the years, especially when I became a sales trainer, and it is obvious why I failed, and why I failed so quickly. First of all, I abandoned the *proven sales template* and developed my own. At the same time, I was "curb judging" people (by their house appearance mostly) who would buy and who would not. I reasoned I could do this from my vast experience and just by looking at the house. I was headed for disaster and since there was no one there to get me back on track, I went down the tubes in a matter of a couple of days. And all this after setting sales records.

Curb judging is a real killer in potential sales. However, not incorporating a proven sales template into your sales presentation and then sticking to it, can be even more deadly.

So how does this all tie into my dealings with farmers for four and a half years? I am glad you asked. The term "Cherry Picking" and "Picking The Low Hanging Fruit" I have mentioned earlier in my book are two interesting and similar terms used in sales, regardless of what you are selling. Let me explain. When you Cherry Pick in sales, you only pick the fruit (qualified customers) that obviously looks good and will most likely be sweet, thereby ending up in a sale.

When you "Pick The Low Hanging Fruit" in sales, it is very similar. You are going after sales that are easy to obtain. In that Fuller Brush job that I had, my relatives would have been considered low hanging fruit and nice looking homes would qualify as cherry picking. In an Amway job or Tupperware rep position years ago, the first sales 99% of the distributors made were to their friends, relatives and neighbors. However, if they did not venture out beyond their *immediate sphere of influence*, they usually became discouraged and eventually quit.

Virtually all salespeople in either an outside or inside sales position must not only move beyond this Cherry Picking and Low Hanging Fruit stage, they must (to borrow some farm terms), till, plant, cultivate, fertilize, grow and harvest crops (or customers) well beyond the initial, easy picking stages. As the farmer saying goes, "you cannot eat your seed or there will be nothing for planting next year". So, with all this in mind, one of the problems I found with distributors and their salespeople was exactly the fact that they would burn up a township quickly by Cherry Picking and/or picking the Low Hanging Fruit and not bother to work the rest of the territory or farmers, in between.

Sometimes with this method, they could set sales records overnight. However, to make matters worse, many of these salespeople and many of the distributors were making so much money compared to what they were making previously, they would spend it all and not reinvest it back into their business (eating your seed corn). The result was inevitable. As they had to start working the rest of their territory, things were not as easy and the money did not roll in as high each week as it had done earlier.

Usually they would contact the home office wanting more territory and we had to decide if they were sweeping through an area quickly, or really working it farm by farm. If they were hitting the Low Hanging Fruit and Cherry Picking, discouragement could set in within a few days, and sometimes I could lose a salesperson so quick, I would never have a chance to save them. In fact, this is exactly what happened to me with the Fuller Brush sales job. I got discouraged so quickly, I was mentally and physically finished within hours, once things started going bad.

<u>Cherry Picking and Low Hanging Fruit does work if your territory is endless and you have no competition. Otherwise, there is a limit to your lucrative and easily found success.</u>

It would amaze me sometimes the incredible sales I would get from farmers whose places looked like a wreck or disaster waiting to happen. Conversely, I would call on farmers whose operation was pristine and they demonstrated all the traits and characteristics of the perfect prospect, only to be turned down flat. Certainly, there are many reasons this is true, but my point is, in sales, we cannot assume who will buy and who will not buy until we check into things below the surface.

All the sales and customer service books I have read, are filled with examples where potential customers with big bucks to spend are overlooked or snubbed by salespeople, especially if they do not

What I Learned In Life From A Liquid Manure Pit

look like a qualified prospect. However, the smart ones know that what appears on the surface is not always what will pan out when some further qualifying work is performed.

I remember driving into a farm once that I could not see very well from the road. There were no beautiful blue tube Harvestor silos or large grain storage bins. There wasn't a nice pole barn either. However, I had learned while chasing farmers down, you could drive right by where they actually lived, constantly missing them out in the five or ten places where they farmed. This place had a house that from the outside needed a good coat of paint five to ten years before I arrived.

There were various types of torn apart farm implements strewn throughout his farmyard. In addition, he had a wooden shed not much bigger than a two-stall garage in today's homes, that looked like it was seconds away from caving in. If the pickup truck had not been in the yard, I probably would have been tempted to make a U-turn and never stop. This farmer comes out of his back door to greet me with a toothpick in his mouth and a big, friendly grin on his face. This is always a good sign in this business, and any business for that matter.

As I got out of my truck he piped up and said in a loud voice… "I wondered if you were going to catch up with me. I heard you were selling those bolt kits and those socket wrench sets to my neighbors, and I was getting worried you would miss me. Hope you got some of those drill bits sets left too cause I break them all the time." I responded enthusiastically… "I have plenty left of everything and there is no way I would miss you. That's why I am here. So, it sounds like you are interested in the whole nine yards like most of your neighbors are buying?" He answered just as enthusiastically… "Yeah, I think I am. Let me see what you've got."

<u>I learned a long time ago in sales that if the customer is sending you incredible buying signals, especially right in the beginning of the sales encounter, go for the close as soon as possible and start right at the top of what you are offering. Like I mentioned earlier, you can always work your way down if need be.</u>

The sale with him was incredibly fast but the talking afterwards was not. He was in no hurry and it was plain to see he liked people, even salespeople. During the sale and after we placed everything in his shed, we talked about a lot of different things covering a wide range of subjects. He also informed me his base operation was the next place down the road where he had a relative renting the house from him. He needed to go into his house to get his checkbook so he invited me in "out of the hot sun" and when I got inside his home, I had to be careful not to show my shock of disbelief.

This place was beautiful inside. Inserted in the dining room window they had a very large BTU window air conditioner that was keeping that entire downstairs cool on a hot August day. His wife was most gracious and her kitchen looked like something out of a magazine. I dare say it would have rivaled most expensive home kitchens of then and maybe even now. We sat down and immediately I was offered a piece of either cherry or apple pie (both favorites of mine), and a refreshing drink of my choice. I chose cold milk if they had it, and they did. I was in instant heaven.

This man and his wife would later become friends enough that when they were in Grand Rapids, Michigan once, we invited them to stop by and we returned their graciousness. Grand Rapids was the home of Amway and they came here for a regional convention. Eventually, this farmer guided me to every viable farmer in the area I had missed, going over the plat book page by page in that wonderful, air-conditioned kitchen. I was offered another piece of pie and I readily accepted it. Besides that, visions of sugarplums were dancing in my head as the plat book pages turned and he circled the farmers I should call on... "and be sure you let them know I sent you." Wow, is this a great country or what? I made sure he was amply rewarded for his extra efforts, even though he at first refused to take anything.

I would be remiss to leave out at least one situation other than the "cob roller" incident in Iowa whereby the farm looked like a million dollars and very advanced, but I did not get the sale. This one was very unique too because I was referred to this farmer by his brother, a county away and referrals are usually a done deal! Immediately I could see he was not the same demeanor of his brother and in fact, I could tell he had three traits that are always tough to overcome, especially on a cold call.

What I Learned In Life From A Liquid Manure Pit

The first trait was that he was a "know it all". The second was that he was a braggart. The third one was that he did not trust salespeople because.. "They are always saying they have the best over the competition and I cannot survive in farming without it. Does it look like I need what you have to be more successful?" Wow, I had not said that or even implied it, but he had already put me on notice. I thought he may have emphasized this because his brother referred me to him and he did not want to appear as an easy sale. After a few moments and a few more attempts to close, I could see this was going nowhere, so I brushed the dust of him and his farm from my clothes and moved on. Some people are just strange and would rather be weird and controlling and miss a good deal than show any weakness whatsoever. There were too many other farmers waiting for what I had to sell.

Cob Rollers are one thing, but people like this can be clients from hell if you continue to pursue them, especially if you are selling something complicated that requires a lot of steps and handholding like building a home for them. I learned to avoid these people in the future like the plague.

I never saw his brother again because that territory eventually was assigned to a distributor. However, back then and in today's sales market now, this kind of guy would tell a salesperson, right or wrong, what he thought and that would be that. You could mirror such a person and maybe get a shot at them, but they are like trying to nail Jell-O to a wall. Keep in mind, I did curb judge him as a great prospect just by the look of his farm as I drove up his drive.

This farmer was an excellent referral from his brother, and from past experience, you know you are going to close those referrals at least 90% of the time or more when you play your cards right. However, he instantly let me know he was not going to continue being a great prospect once we engaged in the sales encounter. Yet everything I saw up to the point of meeting him in person, told me he would be a buyer (and he really should have bought the products, because he did not have what we offered and it would have made his farming life easier and more efficient).

Probably the almost guaranteed "curb judging" sale for me was the farmer with signs that told salesmen to stay away. My favorite was, and I stated this earlier in the my book.... "Salesmen-Beware, we shoot every third salesman and the second one just left." I loved it because this guy had a sense of humor, but some salespeople took these signs seriously. Pristine farmyards and beautiful brick homes were just about a done deal. So were the biggest and the best in the way of farm equipment like massive tractors and large combines, along with shiny new planters, cultivators and an array of other farm implements.

As I continue to sell my own firm's capabilities today, while also training my clients' salespeople in all types of businesses and marketplaces, I teach them to watch for these definite potential *buyer indicators*. However, I also teach them not be fooled by façades that would indicate there will be no sale.

<u>*I was once taught by a friend who was a great salesperson to "Never assume anything in sales, or you may live to regret the assumptions afterwards." To this day, I find myself making sure I do not fall into that trap while training others and while selling myself and my company's benefits.*</u>

Chapter 17

Learning The Value Of Having The Tools You Need In Sales To Not Only Get The Job Done, But To Excel Too

I hate to admit how many times in my early sales career when I came to the sales encounter unprepared. Like my sports career, I did not like to practice or be fully prepared. I just wanted to go out and play, because that was a lot more fun. Sometimes I did all right that way but most of the time this behavior hurt me.

I once attended a sales seminar where the presenter touched on this subject.... "Being unprepared on a sales call with a qualified sales lead can cut your chances of success on that great lead from 30% to as much as 50% or more. In these types of situations, you had better pray the customer is dying to have your product or service, despite your inadequacies. Or you had better hope that you are the only one who has what they want."

What I Learned In Life From A Liquid Manure Pit

He went on to say.... "Practice does not make you perfect, but it does make you permanent in whatever behavior you are doing. Therefore, if you practice the wrong behavior, and keep on with that wrong behavior consistently, soon it becomes a permanent, bad behavior. And when you 'wing it', and 'fly by the seat of your pants', it's like thinking you can walk onto a basketball court or football field without the many hours of drills and practice you need to do first, in order to play well. You are going to lose, guaranteed." Wow, did that hit home with me because up until then, I did a lot of all the above bad behaviors in my sales career, while still doing all right, but not great.

Dealing with farmers would seem simple enough in regards to being prepared. However, like a pilot getting ready to take off with a private airplane, I realized early on, these field reps I had inherited needed a checklist. Most of them were often unprepared and hit the road running on far less cylinders that they could have. Keeping inventories of the hottest selling items was one major problem. It just doesn't work to get a farmer all excited about something and then have to give them a rain check.

Even worse, I would find some salespeople did not mention a hot selling item at all because it was not on their truck and they did not want to come back to deliver it. Boy, did that infuriate me. Of course, some reps spent their money faster than they could make it, so when it came time to restock, they were severely short of cash and went begging for the inventory they should have on hand.

Another problem was not having their truck neat, clean and organized. If you looked good and you could find what you needed when you sold something, it spotlighted you as a professional. On the other hand, when you had to root around looking for things, it did not. Another important tactic I learned earlier in other sales jobs in my career, was to rotate your inventory samples so you did not end up with dog-eared samples you could never sell at list price, once they started looking bad.

For many salespeople and the things they sell, this statement may not relate. However, to those of us in retail sales or direct sales, in the home or in a business, where we carry the product with us, or it is in a showroom, it makes a ton of sense. You never get a second

What I Learned In Life From A Liquid Manure Pit

chance for a first impression....never. So think about how that item you are selling looks to the customer after lots of demos. In the nut, bolt and tool business, we immediately rotated our inventory with every sale so everything looked like it just came out of the box (which of course it did).

In sales, you need to be able to remove yourself from where you are, and look at yourself and what you are doing from the customer's point of view, objectively. In addition, if you cannot pull that off, get a trusted friend to do it for you.

In addition, I would find salespeople who did not want to pay the five or ten dollars for a plat book and they would "wing it" through a township and the county, usually cherry picking along the way. Invariably they would miss great prospects and get turned around easily. That plat book shared incredibly vital information including the name of the owner of the property and the total acres. In addition, it was a great tool to make notes on and keep score. Plus, when you did find an ally who wanted to help you find the other great farmers like them, all you had to do was pull those books out and have at it. They were priceless and when I finally got out of the business, I gave those plat books to the reps who took over my territories.

Besides all those great sales tactics mentioned above, we had sales aids, free give aways, price lists, charged batteries for our filmstrip machine, a restocked cooler and toll free stickers, just to name a few additional things on the checklist. Whenever I worked with a salesperson or a distributor, I made sure they understood that these things were vital to our proven sales template.

Once you start eliminating or forgetting these sales aids and tools, soon your closing ratio starts dropping dramatically. When I would ride with someone whose sales were down and they were hurting, invariably I would find key things eliminated from their sales presentation that were supposed to be part of their proven sales presentation template. Again, this was a lesson I experienced very early in my own sales career with Fuller Brush, I did not appreciate or understand what had happened to me when I quit using the tools of the trade, until many years later.

The only thing worse than dropping key things from your sales presentation is forgetting to use them altogether, or leaving key items or material at home or back at the office. One time I met a salesperson at a small town restaurant early in the morning. While where we met was in the heart of his territory, it was a good 35 miles from his home. We talked about a number of things and he began to get over being nervous in that he would be riding with me that day. Then after breakfast, the problems began. I took a close look at the inside of his truck and he was missing some key items which would cost him sales for the day.

    I asked him if he had them and he said… "Yes, back in my garage but I used my truck over the weekend to help a friend move and in my haste to get going this morning, I must have forgotten to reload those items in there last night." I took some of these items off my truck and had him sign off for them. Then, on the very first call, after a decent sale was made…. you guessed it, he was missing his sales receipt book. Thank goodness I had plenty of them with me, too. Needless to say, this guy did not last long with the company, even though he had some promising sales abilities. He just could never become organized and he always had an excuse. They say "the devil is in the details" and in the sales game, that is a definite truism.

    There is a 1000 year old, anonymous poem, I always share about these vital, little things with my sales force and sales people I train, to help drive this point home. It goes like this: "For want of the Nail, the Shoe was lost. For want of the Shoe, the Horse was lost. For want of the Horse, the Knight was lost. For want of the Knight, the Battle was lost. And for want of the Battle the War was lost."

Chapter 18

Some Additional Reasons And Stories Why I loved Selling To Farmers And Why It Was So Much Fun

As I mentioned earlier in the book, what started out to be a one-year contract, ended up being a four and a half year run at selling to farmers around the country. For virtually most of the time, I was enjoying it fully. What fascinates me to this day is when I am traveling in different parts of the country by truck, automobile or even flying over a particular area I recognize, flashbacks occur in my mind of the farm and the farmer as I go by. Sometimes I need to only come within 50 miles or so of a very memorable farmer and situation before that particular memory kicks in and I start to relive it in my mind.

In my deep dreams and even at times when I am just daydreaming, I focus in on a specific farm, the farmer and the situation, and they seem to show up for no reason whatsoever. Many of these dreams and daydreams, as well as most of my good and bad incidents, are now at the top of my list, in my book, and most have a chapter dedicated to them. The one reason I am sure this occurs repeatedly in my dreams and in my mind and as I travel across the country, is that I really did love what I was doing out there, and the experiences ranged from incredible to unbelievable to mundane. However, eventually, despite the good money that continued to come in, I was ready to do something new. Especially something that focused on my original higher learning and experience of broadcasting and audio/visual knowledge.

__Besides knowing when to hold em, and knowing when to fold em, you need to know when you are just putting in your time and move on to something where you can be totally enthusiastic again.__

When I share some of my stories in seminars or social gatherings, many times so-called city slickers have asked me... "What were these farmers and their families really like?" My response is usually about the same one.... "They were wonderful people for the most part. Their hospitality was second to none. They were usually God-fearing, mom and apple pie type, home cooking people who vehemently defended their country, their rights and their freedom. And by the way, while the country western song had not come out yet with these lyrics, they definitely believed that... "A country boy can survive."

There were Democrats and Republicans out there, as well as more conservative people who belonged to the John Birch Society. Regardless of their party affiliation, conservatism seemed to be the rule of thumb. They wisely supported their congressional representatives who supported them, and especially ones who fought for subsidies and other means of reward for farming. What I am saying is that these people believed they lived in the greatest country on the planet and 99% of them wanted to farm and make it at farming more than anything else. Unfortunately then and over the last fifty years, one by one for financial reasons, death or a potpourri of other causes, these great Americans and their farms began being absorbed by larger farmers and corporate farmers And the need for urban development of the American dream, in rural areas, started taking its toll then and continues to so in a big way today.

They were devoted to family and they loved country western music (it was the older style then but the newer, contemporary style was coming in fast with the younger farmers). They knew we "city slickers" thought of them as "dumb, red necks and hillbillies", but they did not hate us, they just...as one farmer put it to me shortly after I got into this business.... "Consider the source. There is no way you can fully appreciate the farming life if you were raised in the city." I totally agree with that statement because I was a perfect example.

As I explained earlier, there were many times I was invited at the end of the day, to stay at someone's home overnight rather than move on and stay at a hotel. I laugh each time I think of this happening because it has to be where all the farmer's daughter jokes were spawned. I ran into a lot of traveling salesmen out there, but rarely one I would have asked to stay overnight, if I had been the farmer. Therefore I considered it a great honor to be asked to do so.

The first time I gave in was after three requests that I stay. It proved to be a wonderful farm family in the Thumb area of Michigan. This farmer was as nice a person as he could be and he was very religious too. It was towards the end of the day and I would have to drive about 25 miles to the nearest city to book a motel for my first night in the area. Normally I set up at a motel in the center of where I would be operating late Sunday evening or early Monday morning, and then travel out each day from there, always working my way back at night. In this case, I wanted to work this area a bit and then end up at my central point of operations for the week. Therefore, for this reason, I did have my suitcase with me and everything I needed to stay over—no excuses.

Dinner was late as usual because these were dairy farmers and they had a very large herd. The spread for dinner was incredible and whenever I ran into this, I always thought to myself..... "Man, these are hearty people and I continually see them eating like this for breakfast, lunch and dinner. They have a zillion calories to burn off each day." Well, if you watched these people work each day, you would know that they did burn those calories off.

At dinner, it seemed like I got center stage with the questions about how things were going around the country and my responses. I was a celebrity of sorts. I had to be very careful I did not have hoof and mouth disease whenever I did respond. I found out early that if you lied and went along with the crowd, and told them what you wanted them to hear, instead of voicing your real opinion, they would lose interest in you and even question your credibility. It was not that they wanted to argue, they just wanted to hear other points of view besides there own. In addition, they loved hearing the inside scoop about what was happening in farming across the nation, close up and personal. Our company's national sales force and our newsletter kept me on top of what was happening once I became a distributor and quit traveling all over the country.

In Relationship Selling, you must Position yourself as a resource person to your clients, within the marketplace you are serving, and outside of it, if you want to capture "more than your fair share" of the initial sales. Do this consistently and you will maintain your clients for years.

National politics was not that big a deal, unless it was a presidential election year. However, local and state politics usually were a big deal. Watergate happened during my early tenure in this business and lots of speculation of what was going to happen to President Nixon and his cronies really dominated the conversation back then. One thing that really fascinated me was when the High School basketball playoffs started in the state of Indiana, you might as well pack up your gear and move on to a different state. Talk about enthusiasm!

You see, every small town in that state honestly believed that when it came to the state playoffs, regardless of their record, they had a potential state champion. To prove that, all you had to do was stop and go into a gym and read the flags on the wall, or see the signs at the entrance to the school or the city. I did attend a few games whereby farmers had extra tickets and someone could not come at the last minute. Usually they would look at me and say... "You like high school basketball?" My answer was always an enthusiastic "yes" but if the truth were known, I never did like basketball. I guess it was because I could never play the game, even though I was a decent athlete in other sports. However, I must confess that when I would go to a game, they were so spirit filled and hard fought, with both crowds going crazy, you could not help but get involved and love the entire experience.

There is an age-old saying that goes like this… "When in Rome, do as the Romans do." More often than not, it not only helped me bond with that client, but they would introduce me to their friends and you know "The Rest of The Story".

One of the greatest joys in this business was when I stopped back to see a well-satisfied customer six months to a year later. Sometimes, when the original sale went extremely well and they even sent me to other farmer friends, I would make a special, coded mark on the plat book so if my memory failed me, the plat book would not. It was a crude "contact management" program compared to the sophisticated ones we professional sales people use today, but it was very effective and it got the job done.

It would be like "Old Home Week" with some of these people and you honestly felt like family. Sometimes I even got the feeling of what it might have been like to be the Prodigal Son from the Bible's New Testament because there would be one or two sons who busted their butts all year long on the farm, and here comes this Nut and Bolt salesman driving into the yard with an exuberant greeting from their dad. Occasionally it embarrassed me but I never said anything to squelch their father's enthusiasm. The real pay off was that if they had not sent me to someone the first year, I gave them awhile and then I would ask if they knew anyone else who should have this program. Invariably they would and in many cases, they already had one or two names lined up for me to run down before I even asked.

Those follow up sales were like shooting fish in a barrel because usually, that farmer had told my customer for me to call on them when I was back in the area. I really loved making the initial repeat call and the referral call later. However, you know what I loved even more was doubling back to the referral source after the sale was culminated and rewarding them with a small gesture of their kindness to me. In addition, I learned during this part of my sales career life to ask for a referral source's help if a referral they gave me stalled or went sour. It amazed me how they could resurrect a potential sale if you took the time to ask for their help.

<u>Referrals are a Critical Success Factor in professional selling. You need to know when to ask for them, you need to know how to generate them, and you need to know how to take care of a customer or a referral source in a kind way, when you get a referral that culminates in a sale. In addition, don't forget to ask for their help if a referral stalls</u>.

Chapter 19

A Further Sampling Of The Many Great Stories I Love To Share In Seminars, Parties And Other Social Gatherings

There are many stories I share in my seminars and socially that do not hold much, if any sales points within them. They are just fun to tell. For instance, here is one I tell often, usually to a crowd made up mostly by men as you will see why in a moment.

I had loaded up from a Farm Machinery Show with as much as my truck would hold and my assignment was to hit the farmers and ranchers out West in territories not yet covered by a distributor. As I stated earlier in the book, usually the game plan was to make sure you got to the lead first. The second step in the plan was to make sure you had enough product to sell and deliver on the spot to all the farmers or ranchers you (or someone else) saw at the show, and promised you would stop and see.

This was especially critical for people the furthest away from Michigan for me, because if you ran out of product and still had four or five additional sure sales waiting for you, it was too far a distance for me to come back. In addition, chances are, we would not get a distributor to travel a great distance just to get one or two sales. Therefore, there was no cherry picking on the way out to the last farmer or rancher in line. That could be done once you hit all the "almost for sure" sales and were on your way home. That is of course if you still had anything left to sell.

My last stop this time around was a rancher somewhere in Northwest Nebraska. I swear his ranch was so big, it was on the Atlas map. When I finally reached his place by getting last minute directions over the telephone about 50 miles away, I came to a big arched ranch sign with the name of the ranch, built over a cattle guard with roller bar type footing that cattle did not like, so you did not have to have a gate to open and close. To each side of that was barbed wire stretching as far as the eye could see. This rancher had wanted at least one of everything we were selling at the show so I was sure to have at least that much on the truck. He had been friendly on the phone and very pleased I was coming, so I was sure of the sale. The ranch was ten miles from that open gate and when I finally saw the ranch, as I came over a small rise, I was sure I had arrived at the Bonanza Ranch and little Joe was going to run out and greet me.

There was a meandering stream behind the homestead, some additional buildings, cattle in one pen, a good deal of cattle in a field behind the ranch and some horses in another pen. Well, to make a long story short to set up the real story here, the rancher and his wife were very friendly, they treated me like royalty, and he bought at least one of everything I had in addition to some extra bolt and nut refills. Since it was late, they invited me to stay over of course, and quite frankly, since I had not seen a motel in the last 40 miles or more, I readily accepted. In the morning after breakfast, which was fantastic with all the fixings, and a great conversation, they saw me

What I Learned In Life From A Liquid Manure Pit

off and I headed back to the nearest town to fill up both of my 25-gallon gas tanks.

Since he basically cleaned me out of my remaining materials, I was going to head home rather than try to make a few more very small sales stops along the way. He had given me the fastest way to drop down to Highway 80. He pointed out on my Atlas where I could drop south to highway 80 and then head East. I got on that road after filling up both gasoline tanks. And because in those days, gas was very cheap, and my 454 Chevy engine got about eight to nine miles to the gallon fully loaded or empty, I wound her up to about 80 MPH and turned on my CB radio with the squelch wide open.

By turning up the squelch, I would be able to pick up signals from a long way off as well as be able to broadcast out there in the non-interference area. Usually this distance was at least ten miles in any direction, and sometimes much more. I kind of settled into a half sleep on that straight road with no traffic, very content and pleased on this trip and the fantastic money I had made even after expenses. That's when I was jarred out of my wits as a Ford pickup truck went by me as if I was standing still. His wake had actually rocked my empty one-ton Chevy. No sooner had I come to my senses than over my CB radio comes this statement… "Hey, can that Chevy run or not?"

Obviously, I had been challenged to a race and since this highway was straight as an arrow and you could see for ten miles or more in front of you, I took the bait and floored it. Now I must tell you, of the three 454 Chevy Silverado one ton pickup trucks I had while I was in this business, for some reason, this one was the fastest. Bob had also showed me how to flip the cover over on the air filter, supposedly to get just a little better mileage. But mostly, it was to have this loud roar occur when you tromped on the gas pedal and that 454 engine kicked in those carburetors and started to wind out. I had learned to love that sound for some reason and while a 454 engine is not that quick from zero to 60 mph, look out from 60 to 120, because it was like a rocket!

Even though the speedometer did not show it, I knew my truck would do at least 150 MPH if I was not in a strong headwind or going up a steep grade because I had tested it more than once before on long, safe stretches of rural paved highways like this one. This Ford was pulling away from me and he was about a quarter mile ahead when I got up to full speed. It was then that I could see I was gaining ever so slowly on him and I would catch him, and eventually, I might even be able to overtake him.

I got excited because soon I was feeling a buffeting and knew I was entering his draft and I was still ten or so truck lengths behind him. I had never done this kind of thing at these speeds before, but I was thinking that like in NASCAR racing, I could get up real close to the tail end of his truck, and then floor it and get around him (the ole slingshot thing NASCAR drivers called it). So that was my plan as I glanced down at my speedometer needle that was well past the 130 MPH reading and still climbing as I closed the gap.

Wow, once I got within about four or less truck lengths, I actually was able to let up on the gas pedal some because I was now entering his full draft. That convinced me I had all the power I needed to pass him and since no cars or trucks were coming at us for as far as the eye could see, I did not hesitate for long. I pushed the pedal to the floor again and swung out to his left. It was exciting as I began to pass him without much effort. So at first, it was very easy. My adrenalin was pumping big time and I thought I would pass him in just a few seconds or so. However, as I got even and then a little bit ahead of his front bumper, I was now the drafter instead of the draftee.

So the further I got out in front of his front bumper, the slower I was pulling away from him so that I could actually claim victory. I was able to get a full truck length in front of him but that was certainly not a safe distance to try and cut in on him. After this went on back and forth for a few moments with no clear victory on my part and no more pulling ahead, I eased back into his partial draft, a little surprised I had not passed him clearly by now. Keep in mind here for a moment too that I had not seen a North bound vehicle since I got on this highway, and the visibility was good for many miles in any direction. Plus, there were no solid yellow "no passing lines" whatsoever. So neither of us felt any real danger in running side by side at these speeds.

It was then I noticed we had been racing on a very long, slight uphill grade the entire time I was trying to pass him. Wind was not

What I Learned In Life From A Liquid Manure Pit

a factor as it sometimes is on the Great Plains. However, I was sure now this uphill grade was keeping me from passing him clearly. I could see this grade was going to crest soon and then go slightly downhill, within another mile, ever so slightly too. That would help both of us but I figured it would help my more powerful engine the most, giving me a distinct advantage so that I could finally pass him clearly and safely. So I decided I would lay back in his draft and then pass him once we hit the downhill grade.

I was poised to make my move as I could feel us cresting the slight grade and starting downhill. I floored it once again and I could see this time I would be able to pass him safely. I quickly got out ahead of him and was just about to ease over in front of him when, without any warning, it happened. My pickup truck slowed up instantly and dramatically. I did not wear a seat belt in those days so I almost went through the windshield as it felt like someone threw out a big boat anchor behind me, dragging on the road. Racing through my mind was the fact I had blown my engine. No way... not my trusty 454 engine!

By the time I came to my senses and watched him pull away, I looked down at my instrument panel for an oil light or an overheated engine. Everything looked okay at first glance and I did not hear any awful noises coming from under the hood. That's when I suddenly noticed my fuel gauge read empty! I had somehow in this ten to fifteen minute flat out race, gone through 25 gallons of gas on my first tank. And the problem was that in those earlier dual tank models, when you were about to run out of gas or you eventually did run out of gas, you needed to hit a toggle switch under the dash quickly to switch over to the other tank.

If you forgot to switch tanks ahead of time and actually ran a tank dry, you could do it on the run, but you would lose speed instantly in the process. Then it would take less than a second or two for your engine to suck up gasoline from the fresh tank and get you up to speed again. In the meantime, you would slow down fairly fast because that big ole 454 engine demands lots of gasoline to run smoothly and acts as a brake when there is no fuel to feed it. The smart thing was to always switch to the full tank *before* you ran that first tank completely dry. Oh well, not this time.

In this incident, I had sucked that first tank dryer than it had ever been drained! Moreover, at that speed, my 454 engine worked like a vacuum brake of major proportions. I was so happy to flip that switch at about 80 MPH when I realized what had happened. The engine fired up again instantly. Needless to say, I did not try to catch up with him again or I would have run out of gas before I got to Highway 80.

As I got ready to key up my CB microphone to talk to him, he beat me to the punch. He wondered what had happened to me and I told him and then I asked him, "How in the world did you keep going without running out of gas like I did?" He told me he had two tanks. One very large tank and one smaller reserve tank for gasoline. He also had a very large tank in the back of his truck with a hand crank pump for diesel fuel (which was used to refill equipment in the field). I joked that he may be borrowing gas from me before we got to the next town if he didn't slow up and he laughed. We cruised on down to highway 80 talking on our CB's about a lot of things along the way. He even knew the rancher I had stayed with the night before.

We both made it to highway 80 all right, with gas to spare. He pulled into a particular filling station and I followed him. We shook hands and had a few laughs while filling up. Eventually he even admitted I had a wee bit faster truck and of course, he was correct. The bittersweet part of all this was I had to fill up both tanks with gas again and I had only traveled about eighty or so miles. Thank goodness, gas ranged from 29 to 34 cents a gallon in those days, instead of what we are faced with today.

Anytime you get into a contest, and you want to win, and think you can win, make sure you know your limitations and the strengths of the competition that could slow you up or stop you dead in your tracks along the way.

I learned to always set *income* sales goals each week and track them after every sale and kept them in plain view on my dashboard to encourage myself. Reaching goals need specific rewards and my main reward was that when I hit the goal, I was on my way home. Normally I came home Thursday afternoons, but this was late Wednesday afternoon and I had hit my income sales goal. I was

What I Learned In Life From A Liquid Manure Pit

sure I would do so and therefore, I had checked out of the motel that morning before hitting the road selling. Usually, once I hit my goal, I might do some stopping along the way home for a few more sales, if I wanted some extra income above and beyond my goal, but that was rare. I had "the hammer down" and my truck hood worked like a compass pointed to Grand Rapids, Michigan, wherever I might be in the country at the time this happened.

Because the traffic was mostly truckers that afternoon, I was rolling about 10 to 12 miles per hour over the speed limit and I was in the outside lane. The reason I felt so safe was that through talk over my Citizen Band radio, I had what we called back then, "a front door" or a trucker who was letting all of us behind him know if a Smokey Bear or State Trooper was coming at us with radar. If you had a "back door", it was even better. In addition, checking occasionally with a trucker going the opposite direction, improved this system to almost perfection. Usually this system worked very well and once you caught up with your front door, you needed to find another one quickly.

This late afternoon I was rolling across upper Indiana about 30 miles from the Michigan state line and I wanted to have a four-day weekend with my wife Judy. I was feeling good and comfortable in what all of us vets on the road called the "rocking chair" whereby you could relax while speeding because, in effect, everyone was watching out for you. Suddenly I realized I had passed my "front door" trucker I had been having some friendly talk with and immediately I began trying to find a new "front door". I should have slowed up until I found one, but I didn't.

That's when my adrenaline shot to a peak level as I saw a smoky bear in the outside lane going West bound. "Hey" I thought to myself instantly… "Why didn't anyone warn me about this guy?" No sooner had I thought that and he came on his CB and spoke to me very authoritatively… "Hello blue and white Chevy pickup truck with that big CB antenna, I've got you on radar doing fifteen over the limit. I am going to do a flip (which meant he was going to turn around in the median as soon as it was safe for him to do so, and come after me), so pull over right now."

Well, I was approaching an exit. So, I thought to myself... 'Pulling over can also mean getting off the highway altogether on the exit ramp.' So that is what I did. I took awhile to stop on purpose and for that planned reason, I was almost at the end of the ramp, but clearly visible. Again, at the time, in my mind, I was being pragmatic, not criminal. So if he saw me, fine, I would lose some of that great money I had just made and be delayed a bit getting home. On the other hand, if he missed me, maybe I would be able to reason in my mind it was meant to be. Well, there I sat with my adrenaline pumping again, waiting for him to arrive.

I was in plain view though and ready to take my medicine when the trooper eventually spotted me. But that's when I heard a lot of trucker chatter on my CB radio saying I was headed "Eastbound with the hammer down". As it turned out, they were basically filling the channel with false information for the trooper! In addition, because of this malicious chatter, I am convinced that trooper was using his private police channel radio to alert fellow officers to look for me coming their way. I was waiting for him to arrive, see me at the end of the ramp, and write me up with that expensive ticket. However, to my amazement, he roared right by that exit at an extremely high rate of speed with his lights flashing big time and his siren howling. How in the world had he missed me on the ramp? I reasoned the truckers caused this to happen, *not me*.

There was no gloating or feeling like I had outsmarted this trooper. In fact, I was scared to death and realized I would be in really big trouble when they caught up with me because as far as

What I Learned In Life From A Liquid Manure Pit

he was concerned, from the trucker chatter, I was trying to outrun him. My heart was pumping like crazy. Now I did feel like a real criminal. I decided to just sit there for a while and let my heart slow down and allow my adrenaline to back off until I figured out what to do next. I was faced with a real fear and a real dilemma... 'How was I going to get home without being caught?' My mind played crazy games as I was sure there was by now, a major manhunt going on, with hundreds of troopers looking for me while watching the state line. And when they caught up with me, I just knew they would lock me up and throw away the key. My only alternative was to continue off the exit and take the back roads home to Michigan. I had worked this area for a long time so I knew every single one of them like the back of my hand.

It took me a couple of hours longer to get home that evening but I made it without incident and got back on the main highways once I was well into Michigan. However, when it came time to work again the following week, I decided I needed to work in another territory where I would not have to go through that trooper's area again. It took me over a month to finally feel comfortable enough to use the main interstate highway through my territory and whenever I saw a trooper going the other way, or heard one was coming up behind me, I cringed, waiting for him to recognize me and pull me over.

Eventually, I quit worrying about the incident, because I knew all the trooper had was a general description of my truck at a distance. I also knew there was no way he had gotten my license plate. However, I never forgot that incident and it is not a story I share very often. As I said, no one had gotten my license plate number, but my truck was beautiful and it stood out in the crowd. One thing this incident did do was to discipline me from that day forward, never to run more than four mph over the speed limit when I was on a super highway, unless I had to get out of the way of someone while being in the passing lane, or I had to speed up to pass someone.

<u>It is OK to have income sales goals, but when it fogs your good judgment as you pursue them, you need to reassess what's important overall.</u>

I love animals and I ran into every type of farm animal you would ever think you would see on a farm in those 4 ½ years of selling to farmers. Of course dairy cows, beef cattle, hogs, sheep, turkeys and chickens topped the list. I also got to know the watchdogs of farms called peacocks. These animals strutted around when you arrived and gave off a loud, annoying call you could probably hear a mile away and that was the idea. Once in awhile I also saw llamas and even a deer farm now and then.

Of course, I ran over many different types of animals by accident, including my share of raccoons, armadillos, possums, squirrels, rabbits and cats, but for some reason, though I had some close calls, I never ran over a dog. Another amazing thing is with all those hundreds of thousands of miles traveled, I never hit a deer or cow, even though I came close to hitting deer numerous times.

One time I nearly killed myself out West as I came over a crest of a hill going excessively fast in *open range* country were cattle ranged free back then. There were signs that warned you now and then but I did not think too much of it because my visibility was always very good ahead of me. But not this time. There in the middle of the road were beef cattle and I had one small opening to get through and that would have required me leaving the road and not losing control in the process. I never could have stopped in time so once again, God spared me as I flew past them, blaring my horn at around fifty miles per hour versus the seventy I was doing just a few seconds earlier. Had there been a deep ditch or trees just off the road, I most likely would have been killed or severely injured by taking either the ditch or cow choice. That taught me a lesson about traveling too fast in open range country.

I have loved cats since I was a small child and cats seemed to be on most farms. And on dairy farms they were thick as thieves. I accidentally rolled over some kittens in farmyards now and then, but never adult cats. It always broke my heart but farmers were so used to it and they had so many cats, they did not give it much thought.

However, one dumb thing adult cats would do is while you were talking to the farmer and the weather was cold, they would climb up into your engine cowling area to get warm. Once I was done, I would jump in my truck and fire it up and cats would come flying out. However, every now and then, the belts of my engine took their head, paws, or tail off instantly. I always felt so bad when these

What I Learned In Life From A Liquid Manure Pit

things happened but again, the farmers would always shrug it off as no big deal to make me feel better. After this happened a few times, I got to where, when it was cold and cats were in the farmyard as I arrived, when I was ready to leave, I would hammer my hand hard a number of times on the hood before I fired the engine up. That seemed to work. No more dismembered cats for the rest of my career.

Dogs were very common and there were all kinds of dogs. There were the friendly ones who would not leave you alone wanting you to pet them. The only bad thing about them was they also liked to jump on the side of my truck and scratch my paint. Yet, I really liked these types most of all and made over them and actually talked to them like kids. Sometimes, believe it or not, if I knew they were acting like big kids, wagging their tales and presenting an honest to goodness smile on their faces, I would actually lean down and let them lick my face a bit. Funny how the ice was broken instantly when you did that with a farmer's dog that he loved dearly. The real key was to not wipe your face at that point. It may seem gross, but I never left such a situation without some kind of sale.

I did this move sparingly because you knew that dog's tongue had been somewhere else just recently, that you would not have wanted to know about. Some of these really friendly ones usually jumped all over you or nudged your crouch so hard with a sharp, upward movement with their nose, you nearly bent over recovering from the pain. That's when the farmer would yell a very loud... "Buster, get outta there!!!" ...usually taking a mock swing at them in the process. By the way, all dogs had that ritual of sniffing your tires and then peeing on them.

Then you had the barkers that liked to charge you and bluff you, but if you did a short run at them, they panicked and took off quickly into a retreat. You just needed to instantly size up the dogs and never, never show fear of any kind. The ones you had to watch out for were the very aggressive ones. They would bite you if they got a chance and in my tenure of selling to farmers, I was only bitten three times in four and a half years. Two of the dogs I never saw as I went up to the backdoor to knock. One dog bit me high on my shin but I wore cowboy boots, so I felt him hit, but I was not hurt and I ran him off easily.

Then there was the incident I had with a mixed breed dog, about the size of a full-grown Golden Retriever that looked like it had some German Shepard blood in him too. I never saw him either as I was knocking on the backdoor of a farmhouse with no pickup truck in the yard. He snuck up on me and nailed me just above my boot, in the fatty part of my shin. It hurt so bad it brought tears to my eyes.

However, it scared me even more because I never heard or saw him until he bit me. I was sure he had drawn blood. I was hurt and mad now too. I fended him off by quickly taking my cowboy belt off. It was a tactic I had used a few times before. It had a big, heavy buckle, and I was swinging it at him as hard as I could, hitting him once right in the nose. That got him to retreat but not far. I got back to the truck, made sure he was far enough away, and then jumped into the cab. He was growling and jumping on the door now so I decided to take a calculated risk to get even.

I looked around one more time to make sure no one was home. Then I reached under the seat and pulled out my 357-magnum pistol, which was always loaded as you might recall me stating earlier. I was not going to kill the dog, but I was going to scare him to death if I could get the chance. For the second time I checked to make sure no one was home and then proceeded to roll down my window half way and waited for his next snarling lunge.

At that point, as he was in mid air of his next jump, I quickly let off two rounds from that pistol right near his head. That dog did a complete somersault in mid air as he came down off of my door. He was off running instantly and yelping at the same time so I stepped out of the truck and shot off a couple of more rounds over his head for good measure. Unfortunately, my ears were ringing for days because whenever I did target practice, especially with this gun, I wore ear protection and I had not thought of that at the time.

The corn at his farm had not been harvested yet and it was very high. Therefore, except for the immediate farmyard, no one could have seen me do this and I was sure no one was home. Then I realized how foolish this stunt was for various reasons. First of all, doing this and being seen or caught at it, even if it was the dogs fault,

What I Learned In Life From A Liquid Manure Pit

would have been very serious. Second of all, I was not sure yet if he had drawn blood and what if he were rabid? In addition, having not seen a Beware of Dog sign, this could very well be a rabid, wild dog, wandering about the county. In fact, over the years throughout this country, I had run across hunting parties of farmers going after wild packs of dogs that were originally domesticated.

I carefully pulled down my pants now and was relieved to see that in some freak way, the Levis, which were fairly new, and my long underwear, which I had worn for the first time this week, had allowed definite teeth marks to show up on my leg (with a bad bruise later), but to my surprise, no blood had been drawn, just deep red marks. Believe it or not, since it was a lucrative farm, two days later as I was pretty much done with the area, I thought I would stop there again. And this time there was a pickup truck in the yard.

I got out but I was all eyes and ears in every direction this time, looking for that dog as I walked to the back door again. The farmer came out of the house and we talked a bit and I managed to tell him I had been there previously and had a little bit of a run in with his dog (never saying what actually happened). Well, he told me he did not have a dog but he had heard about a wild dog in the area, but he had never seen it. I then told him what actually happened and he said… "Man, too bad you didn't shoot it. Did he draw blood?" Now he tells me. I could have nailed that dog easily but even though he hurt me, my heart just was not in it at the time. However, with the wild dog story interjected into the situation, I would not have hesitated for an instant had I known this ahead of time.

The strangest dog story occurred when I was looking for a very large farmer who everyone I met, told me he would buy what I had, especially if he knew others had it. The reason was simple. Farmers like this liked to always be one-step ahead of everyone else and if this guy saw farmers buying something he did not have, he had to get it right away, and the bigger the better. My kind of customer indeed.

I was operating in a predominately grain farming county and all the crops were in now. That made it a perfect time to call on farmers. I had missed him a few times so one day I asked his wife where I might find him and she told me exactly where to find him in town, at a particular hangout for farmers near the town grain elevator. I asked how I would know him and she said...... "Oh you'll know him all right. He'll have the biggest, loudest mouth in the place and if he is there, his blue Ford pickup truck will be in front of the place and his dog 'Killer' will be in the back of it waiting for him." Well off I went, never thinking twice about the name of the dog.... 'Killer'.

<u>Just when I thought I was a pro at listening and observing those red flags, another one slipped by me as you will see as you read on</u>.

Sure enough, when I arrived in town and found the breakfast hangout, there sat the blue Ford pickup truck with a really friendly looking German Sheppard sitting faithfully in the back of the truck, tail wagging and staring at the front door of the restaurant. He was whining a bid too. I parked near his truck, made sure I had lots of invoices hanging out of my shirt pocket, and proceeded to walk into the place, which was fairly busy at the time.

As luck would have it, since I had really been working this township hard lately, some of my new customers were present and they either waved or nodded acknowledgement as I walked into the restaurant. This farmer was facing me as I entered and talking loud just like his wife had predicted. He was a big man well over six feet and I guessed well over 300 pounds too. He was also aware I had come into the place and he kept talking as his eyes followed me approaching him. Like the old Western movies where the stranger walks into the bar and everyone takes notice, in a small town like this one, with my cowboy dress persona, all eyes and ears were on me. And I swear to you, like in the movies, the place got deathly silent, except for him still talking.

I took a chance and walked right up to him and said.... "Mr. Johnson, a lot of your friends tell me you would be interested in what I'm selling and I thought to make it easy on you, I would come to you here in town and show you what I've got." He was a little taken back by my bold approach, but I could see his eyes check me over quickly, and I could tell he admired that type of boldness in a person. Then I saw his eyes look at those tons of invoices bulging out of my shirt pocket, and he said.... "So what is it you have that is so important?"

At that point, one of the other farmers sitting at his table told him I was the guy selling nut and bolt kits and replaceable drill bits (he added he had bought some from me two days ago). Without further hesitation, he agreed to come take a look and followed me outside to my truck. It only took a few moments and I could tell peer pressure alone, would make this deal happen. In fact, he started wheeling and dealing with me right from the start. He wanted to know if he were to buy one of everything I had, what kind of deal would I give him. I knew I was going to make a lot of money on the deal so I made him a firm but fair offer, and then I shut up. He said that was not good enough and I told him "nobody else has gotten this kind of deal so just keep it between us."

He paused for a moment and then said… "Okay, I will take it all." Knowing guys like this, I was sure he would brag about "holding me up" and taking advantage of me on a great deal later to his buddies, which was peanuts in cost to me, bottom line. However, I always had ways to handle that situation when and if it came up later with farmers in the area I had not called on yet, who heard about his bragging. I would just say…. "Hey you know him and what he is like. What else would you expect him to say? I bet he has told some of his friends he got that nut and bolt set for next to nothing." Well anyway, he wrote me a check and then said…"Put everything in the back of my pickup truck. I've got to pay for my breakfast before I leave, and say goodbye to the boys."

<u>One interesting note here, I cannot remember how many times I sold something to someone where, when the sale was complete, they had to ask me how much they owed me, especially in this farming business.</u> <u>When that happened, you had sold value first and price second, which was and always is the right approach</u>*.*

Well, I had completely forgotten Killer's name by now, so I prepared this man's entire order, making sure I did not forget anything, and then decided to carry the heaviest bolt kit first, and place it flat on the bottom of the bed of the truck. Killer had been watching the two of us talk the entire time, waging his tail and whining now and then. Occasionally the farmer would say… "Killer, shut up!" and he would just whine and do a couple of turn arounds in the bed of the truck, and then continue watching us some more.

What I Learned In Life From A Liquid Manure Pit

Once the farmer returned to the restaurant, I could see Killer was once again fixated on the door of the restaurant. This small bolt kit was heavy but it was still in its shipping cardboard box so I carried it over to the back of the truck, balanced it on one leg on the back bumper, and proceeded to open the tailgate with my right hand, which was free at the time. Never for a moment did I worry about the friendly dog named Killer. That was a big mistake.

No sooner had I dropped open that tailgate and started to slide that bolt kit onto the back bed of the truck and Killer charged and chomped down on my right arm bicep and held fast with his nose and eyes inches from my exposed throat. He was growling a muffled growl. It felt like a big vise had a hold of me and even with my long underwear, a wool long sleeve shirt and a heavily wool lined leather coat, I could feel the pain right into my bones. It happened so fast I could hardly react when the farmer came outside and shouted… "Killer, let that guy alone!"

At this point, he let go instantly and even though he had only held my arm for a few seconds, it felt like someone had taken a hammer to my arm in a 360-degree circle. "Sorry he scared yah a bit. You're okay aren't yah?"….. he asked as I instinctively rubbed my now sore arm. "Oh yeh, nothing serious, he just scared me more than anything." I answered. At that point, I went to get more stuff to load in the back of his truck, knowing I was not going to get too close to Killer on these next trips.

That's when my new customer said in an almost braggadocios manner…. "Yeah, sorry about that. I trained him a long time ago to guard this truck. I forgot to call him off before I went back into the restaurant."

Great, what a brilliant move that was. Thank you very much I thought to myself. To this day, I do not know if he set me up for his personal, sadistic amusement or not, but I will tell you this for sure. My arm was in excruciating pain by that evening and I had to ice it down. I have never bruised easily but my arm became black and blue that night back at the motel. When I got home later that week, the swelling was gone, but the bruise remained and there was a faint outline of teeth marks. I had to keep reminding myself I was not

What I Learned In Life From A Liquid Manure Pit

permanently hurt and I had made a great deal of money from the man, even with a little bargaining.

One more thing about dogs. Whenever I saw a sign that said.... "Beware of dogs", I would psych myself up to not be afraid and that worked repeatedly because the dogs just knew you were not afraid. The dogs would come charging and I would wade through them as if I was one of the family. Now I never did this unless the farmer was right there to call them off. Again, at no time in those obvious situations where I might be bit, did I ever get bitten. I am convinced, dogs just sense fear as well as confidence. Of course, that wild dog I ran into was a totally different matter.

So one time I pulled up to the back door of this place and the signs were a bit different. There were the usual beware of dogs signs as you came up their drive, but there was something new I had never seen before or since. The hand painted sign at the end of the walk to the backdoor said... "Honk your horn. Do Not get out of your car."

Well, for the life of me, I cannot tell you what possessed me to do this, but I pulled up to that farmyard, turned around so my cab door was right near the walk to the backdoor of the house, and proceeded to exit my truck with vicious dogs all around. I had noticed three pickups in the yard, so somebody was home. In addition, I thought I saw some people through the kitchen window, looking out at me. However, there were some very mean dogs jumping at the driver side of the door now as I opened it.

The next thing you know, I did an insane move and I jumped down to the ground and proceeded to walk to the backdoor! These dogs went ballistic when I did that because I think this had never happened before. Next, they began savagely fighting and biting each other right in front of me, leaving me completely alone. Instantly I thought to myself... "What in the heck are you doing Stan? You are in the middle of a three dogs fighting and it's a vicious fight at that. Back up and get inside that truck cab and wait for somebody to come out of the house like the sign said."

This was not a red flag thing; this was pure stupidity and over confidence to boot.

I think that maybe I was in a state of temporary shock now. My over confidence of not being afraid of dogs and having had a fantastic sales day and week up to this point, had dulled my normal intelligence and allowed me to really push the envelope. It was at that point a farmer in his fifties came running out of the backdoor shouting at the dogs with a big, thick broomstick (without the broom) in his right hand. He was screaming at the dogs and calling them by name, while smacking them hard. I think I heard him cursing at me under his breath at the same time. "Oh boy," I thought to myself, "this is not going to be pretty. His dogs are ripping each other apart all because I did not follow the rules."

He calmed the dogs almost instantly after those few well landed hard hits on their heads and rumps and then when he was no more than a few feet from me he said in a very stern, aggravated, cussing voice.... "Good God man, can't you read?" I apologized and told him I had been doing this for many years all over the country and was not afraid of dogs one bit. He looked at me, shook his head and said a few more cuss words under his breath. The he said.... "That is the first and only time anyone but family has gotten out among those dogs without waiting for one of us to call them off. You are either the bravest SOB I have ever met or the craziest."

Then, without skipping a beat he said with every third word a cuss word..... "Obviously you are selling something. What the hell you got?" Well, I didn't waste any time and I proceeded to talk to him a bit about what I had. Suddenly I realized one of these vicious dogs he called Jake, was sniffing me over while the other two were peeing on my tires (a very common thing for farmyard dogs to do by the way). They were still upset and barking a low bark for no reason other than because this idiot had totally changed their world and routine in an instant.

But soon they settled down to regular type dogs within no more than two or three moments at best. The son of this farmer came out later and between the two of them, they bought much of what I had to offer after about a half hour. I thanked them for their business and as I got in my truck to back up and turn around, the dogs went ballistic again and I could see the father hitting them with that broomstick. I only saw that kind of sign once and if I had ever seen it again, I probably would have honked the horn and waited for someone to come from the house.

Epilogue

What a ride this four and a half years of selling to farmers was for me. I learned more about dealing with people and more about sales during that period than I had before or since. I was able to see and experience this great country of ours close up and personal, and I was able to meet some of the most wonderful people in the world, the American farmer and their families. As you can tell by now, having read the book to this point, my experiences were priceless and incredibly diversified. I convinced myself by the end of the second year that "if it could happen, it would happen to me" and it did. There are so many more fun and interesting stories and vignettes I could share, but the book needs to wrap up somewhere. I also thank my Lord and Savior Jesus Christ for saving me physically in my harrowing experiences, and eternally through His Grace.

The trips my wife and I went on due to my sales achievements, took us overseas to Europe for the first time, at a very young age. It also allowed us to be on a luxury cruise, as well as visit islands in the Caribbean and other points of interest throughout this great country of ours. I must admit it was not always fun or total peaches and cream. In addition, because of all the travel I had to do and being alone on the road a lot, I nearly lost my wife through a separation and her eventually filing for a divorce in the middle of my career of selling to farmers. The two of us can thank the good Lord for getting us through that tough time in our lives and back together. And yet, I can honestly say, most of the time I spent in this business was a lot of fun and if I had to do it over again, I would not hesitate for a moment. In fact, I would go into it much smarter and probably make even more money than I did before.

Speaking of money, since I had never been self employed until I got into this business, I was a poor money manager. I was not real good at keeping up with my quarterly payments and this was during the time when the tax code was set up so that you really did get hit harder and harder, tax wise, as you made more and more money. You can imagine my shock the first year in business when my CPA informed me I owed the government thousands of additional tax dollars I had not counted on, including a nice little penalty for not having paid in enough over the course of the tax year.

During those four and a half years, I witnessed first hand the shrinking of the total number of farmers nationwide. It was slow at first but I could see the trend developing. Because farmers took great chances and operated on the whims of Mother Nature, they were usually financed to the hilt when they first started out (and some were stretched to the limit financially all the time).

I remember one time calling on a farmer who had a magnificent farm. We got to talking about the risks involved and he shared with me that while he had over a million dollars of land and equipment (which was a lot then and even now), he was only making interest payments while he slowly tried to pay down the principal. And yet he said…. "But you have to keep growing so I buy and lease land every chance I get because it will never go down in value and we have less and less of it to farm each year."

What I Learned In Life From A Liquid Manure Pit

At that time as I recall, the average farmer in America who was farming regular grain crops, instead of specialty type crops like tobacco or certain vegetables, usually had around 300 to 400 acres. Hobby farmers were those that had a day job and farmed about 80 to 100 acres or less, nights and weekends. The only almost guaranteed secret to success I saw was when your father, and his father before him, had been an extremely successful farmer before you and he had taught you how to be the same. Then, when he was ready to retire, he would pass some or all of the land along to the son or sons to farm and he would take his well-made investments and savings and retire. This allowed that new farmer to enter the farming market with very little owed to the bank and lots of collateral if he wanted to grow cautiously.

As I reflect back, I remember all that equipment you had to own to make things happen on a farm. There were plenty of dangers too in that OSHA really did not have any jurisdiction out in farm country, and if they did, they never could have policed it. Therefore, if you were not constantly aware of your surroundings and what was taking place, an operating piece of machinery could take an arm or leg or kill you altogether. Livestock was still another matter of concern and while I had some stupid self-induced incidents, there were plenty of incidents I heard about that happened to seasoned farmers and ranchers. Then there were those freak accidents you never knew were going to take place.

One time I came upon a farm twenty minutes after the farmer had electrocuted himself. It was one of the worst things I had ever seen in my life and I witnessed many awful accidents on the road during that four and a half year period, where people were torn apart due to highway accidents. The volunteer firemen were there and an ambulance had just arrived but there wasn't anything they could do. His body had literally been fried to a crisp and the stench was a smell I will never forget.

Somehow, he had inadvertently backed into and come in contact with a pole holding a high voltage wire. He was apparently maneuvering a large combine but no one at the time knew exactly what had taken place. They could only speculate that when he forgot about the power pole and inadvertently backed into it, the pole went down instantly and it was further speculated that as he jumped out of the cab of his combine, the high voltage wire hit him and grounded at the same time. It must have been over in a millisecond. His wife had witnessed the entire event and she was hysterical. He was not a customer of mine but the tragedy hit that area so bad, I decided to move a county over and give it time to pass. I did find out though that soon everyone within a 200 mile radius knew about the accident due to television and newspaper reporting of the incident.

Of course, I had bizarre things happen to me that were totally unexpected too, some of which you have read about in previous chapters. I once hired a man in his fifties who had been out of work for over a year. He was probably 60 pounds overweight but he was doing great the first week traveling with me and by midweek, he had made more money than he had made with odd jobs for the last three months. He was incredibly excited and at dinner that Wednesday evening, he called home to tell his wife and family he had found something he could excel at and loved what he was doing.

That night it rained and we were rooming together to save money so after a little TV, we both hit the hay and I said I would get up first around six in the morning. I also told him we would do even better tomorrow because when it rains, farmers are not working in the field and we will catch a lot more of them home or chase them down in town.

He was very quiet during the night after snoring a bit like he had done Monday and Tuesday night. I would holler at him to turn over and the snoring would stop until I was able to get to sleep again. I got up the next morning as planned and did not turn on the lights until I got in the bathroom. It was still very dark out as I showered and shaved. When I came out of the bathroom, I flipped on the main room light and within seconds, I fell to my knees in shock. He was lying on his back, with his eyes and mouth wide open. His blood had drained to the bottom of his body looking very purple.

As I prayed, I reached up and closed his eyes with my left hand. Then I called the office but I did not get an answer. I threw on my clothes and ran to the office in a total state of shock. I must have been incredibly incoherent because I was standing at their door totally drenched and they kept trying to get me to slow down and cipher

What I Learned In Life From A Liquid Manure Pit

out what had happened. When it finally hit them what I was telling them, they called the local police. I guess the police contacted the coroner and the state police because they both arrived shortly after the local police did.

I was questioned by the trooper just to make sure there had been no foul play or anything unusual that had happened between us. Later I was allowed to call my wife and then I had to make the awful call to his wife. Arrangements were made for friends to drive up in a car and then drive the two pickup trucks back to Grand Rapids. I rode in the back of the car with my wife and was trying to sort out what had just taken place. When I finally got back home, my neighbors had decided to keep me up practically all night to help me get through the shock.

It worked wonders and eventually, I fell asleep exhausted and slept for almost 24 hours. Later that week at the funeral, the family let me know they were so appreciative of me giving this man his dignity back. That helped me get over the incident more than anything did, even if the event did haunt me for the next couple of years whenever I roomed with a salesperson. It also gave be some satisfaction to give them the sizeable amount of cash this man had earned in just three days.

To this day, like reciting my ABC's or well-known verses from poems or the Bible, I can remember the nut and bolt sales pitch template I used repeatedly on each sale. Sure, I would customize the rest of the presentation, but as I learned a long time ago with the college Fuller Brush job, to obtain more sales, you did not get away from the proven sales template or you would quickly be in deep trouble. In addition, whenever something came along that could improve upon the sales pitch template, we all shared it with each other through the company newsletter and national sales meetings.

I am sure once this book gets published and gets known across the country, many farmers still around will vaguely remember that nut and bolt salesman with the cowboy hat and the sharp blue and white, 454 Chevy Silverado, one ton pickup truck with the flags on the side (my last two years I had a double cab Silverado which was even more impressive). When I first got into the business and met some distributors, they had what I would call fender flappers or Junker type trucks that had way too much rust and looked like they were on their last legs. Bob, the owner of the company and I agreed with the reasoning that successful farmers wanted to deal with successful people. Many salespeople thought otherwise and their sales reflected this incorrect thinking process.

I admire, love and respect the American farmer and his family to this day and always will. Anytime I am in a restaurant where farmers gather, I make it a point to walk over and talk to them "in their language" and they love it. Very few people outside of the farming community really understand what they go through to make a living and the old days of the average country farm are basically gone. I am so pleased the good Lord allowed me to work with these people, and live to write this story. Another thing I am very appreciative of is the fact that I got to work with the American farmer when they were at their prime in this country and modernization of the industry was at its peak too. God bless them and their families.

While they and their families today probably represent less than a few million people in this country, they feed all of us and they feed a lot of the world today too. My one prayer is that the smaller farmer does not vanish to the absorption of the corporate farm, just like the big box stores and major super markets eliminated the mom and pop corner grocery stores and hardware stores. If this happens, and it appears it will, our nation will have experienced a great loss.

Be Blessed. Stan Barnes

Printed in the United States
212284BV00002B/1/P